YOUR FINANCIAL FLIGHT PLAN

TANYA IBBERSON

authors
AND CO.

CONTENTS

PREFACE – HOW THE GET THE MOST OUT OF THIS BOOK

Hey there! It's lovely to meet you, and firstly, I want to thank you from the bottom of my heart for choosing to read my book. I know there is a huge amount of choice out there, so I'm feeling very privileged that I've made the cut for you. I hope you enjoy it and that you get a lot from it.

My goal is to help as many people as possible to feel worthy of having the financial future of their dreams. The toolkit I share with you isn't all about the finances; it brings in all key aspects to consider, ensuring you have stable foundations in place to support growth and scaling to achieve what you set out to.

It's been written in a certain order; the system that I have created covers specific areas that are best tackled the way it was intended, in my experience. I'm obviously not going to be standing over you as you read this though, so you can, of course, choose to work through whichever chapter order you please.

We start off quite chatty; I want you to get to know me and trust me when I say that the way this has been written is pretty much how I talk. Minus the swearing!

The first two chapters are my promise to you, and a demonstration of my trust in you by sharing my story. I came up with the core concept of this book over years and years of working with clients in my capacity as an accountant, as well as clawing myself out of, what felt at the time, to be an impossible financial situation.

Then I take you through five chapters that cover my trademarked system, the MATHS® system. Included in these are lots of practical advice, guidance, and tips on how to review and analyse what you currently have and don't have in place in your business right now, how to identify bottlenecks and gaps and what you can do about it as the CEO of your empire. I recommend a read through the whole thing first, and then use it as a reference book to cherry pick the parts you want to refer to as you're putting the strategies and advice into practice. I mention the book resource page of my website throughout, so you can access a number of templates, checklists, and other goodies in there, for free. Check out the final chapter for how to access them.

I wrap up in the last chapter with next steps and how you can work with me if that's something you want to learn more about. I have a website and social media accounts, so do feel free to follow me for more content. I look forward to taking this journey with you!

Website – www.financialwingwoman.com

Facebook –

https://www.facebook.com/tanya.matheson2/

Free Facebook Group –

https://www.facebook.com/groups/thelollylounge

Instagram –

https://www.instagram.com/thefinancialwingwoman/

LinkedIn –

https://www.linkedin.com/in/tanya-ibberson-07704419/

In a nutshell, this book is about empowerment, taking back control and acknowledging when change is needed. Whilst it won't be easy, you'll know that with a structure in place, you can absolutely do this and build a flight plan for the life you want to start living right now.

Recent client testimonials (2021/2022)

In the short time that I have known Tanya, she has honestly changed my life more than I could have ever imagined. I have always had a really poor money mindset, and pretty much just earned what I could and hoped for the best, never wanting to look properly at my numbers because they pretty much scared the shizzle out of me. And this made me feel embarrassed. Because as an entrepreneur, I am supposed to know what is going on in my business, because if I don't, then who will?

Tanya isn't like any other accountant I have ever met, she made me feel comfortable and safe enough to share my worries, and then talked to me about them in language I understood. She didn't baffle me with big words, or make me feel like I wasn't doing things right, she asked me questions and reassured me that there was actually nothing to worry about. Tanya showed me that when we can SEE clearly what is happening, then we can take any action that is needed to fill in the gaps, and start planning for all the BIG things in life that we dream of having.

I feel so much lighter, and confident and even EXCITED about where I am going now. I know exactly what is happening, when, and when client's payments to me finish so that I know when and what I need to plan. Tanya is SOOOOO much more than just an accountant. I feel in control of my business for the first time ever, not like I am winging it anymore. Because (this is a bit cheezy sorry, but I am saying it anyway) with Tanya as my Financial Wing Woman, I will NEVER be winging it again.

NIKI KINSELLA, SACRED SPACE HOLISTICS LTD

I have been self-employed since 2015 and in 2019 I was upset that my accountant was not doing what he should but I could not figure out what!!! Tanya was nearby and offered to 'take a look'. We had met through mutual interests and I jumped at the chance for someone to help me. I really had no idea what I was doing with the 'business' but was busy 'doing the do's' with no real idea of what I needed to do for the future.

Tanya has been life-changing for me and my business. Tanya recognised very early on that we needed to follow a systematic process of dealing with one section at a time. If not, I was going to get overwhelmed (tbh, I already was). We tackled one aspect of my business at a time to then get to a point where we could plan what's next!

Over the last 3 years Tanya has turned my business into a stream-lined, well-functioning venture where the possibilities are endless. We have more planning to do and I'm so excited for the future. With Tanya by my side I know I will succeed.

Tanya's kindness and patient approach has meant that I have always felt supported and no question has ever been a problem. Tanya's knowledge and mentoring has been invaluable and I look forward to the future.

SARAH SEMILORE, SARAH SEEKINS CONSULTANCY LTD

Content Disclaimer

The information contained in this book is provided for information purposes only. The contents of this book are not intended to amount to advice and you should not rely on any of the contents of this book for your own personal or business circumstances. Professional advice should be obtained before taking or refraining from taking any action as a result of the contents of this book. Tanya Ibberson and Financial Wingwoman Ltd both disclaim all liability and responsibility arising from any reliance placed on any of the contents of this book.

1

THE INTRODUCTION

To all the people with their head in the game.

To all the people who know they're onto a good thing.

To all the people who are loving the work they do.

To all the people who've found what they were meant to be doing in life.

And to all the individuals who pull it together and are bossing every day.

You know I'm talking to you. You're showing up continuously, spinning all the plates. Not dropping a single one.

I'm speaking to you. I see you.

I know everything about you.

Are you listening? Because this is for you.

You are on the way UP!

You know, deep down, that you're on top of your game. You've found a gap in the market and you're owning it. Doing it differently to everyone else. The work you do in your business is changing lives. You are absolutely on the trajectory to greatness. You are quite literally re-moulding the landscape for so many people and it feels good. Your clients rave about you. They are your biggest advocates and cheerlead you daily. Whether it's talking about you on social media, or recommending you to friends. No, not just friends, they bring you into their family. You are a part of their circle now.

Let me tell you, no one does that for just anyone, but they will for you. And they'll think nothing of it, because they trust you to help and work with their nearest and dearest and you feel honoured. Because you know deep down you are just bringing who you are to the table. Wholeheartedly, unequivocally, and 100% you. You are determined to always bring your A-game and let me tell you, that's what makes you so special. It's why people love you and come back to you again and again. Because whether you know it or not, you're the obvious choice for so many. You tick all the boxes and more than that, you genuinely care about the work you do and the difference you can make for people - and it shows.

So maybe, on the outside, you look amazingly put together, you know how to show up and bring the fire, you get stuff done and you are the wingwoman for your clients and the people around you. You've got a great car, a fabulous wardrobe, and a designer handbag or two (okay, maybe it's an addiction). And picking up a few rounds of cocktails, or a good meal out at your favourite restaurant on date night doesn't have you batting an eyelid.

But there's a catch. Because that's all easy. That serves others. Sometimes, that feels like a facade. Yes, you care. Of course you do. More than anything. However, underneath it all, you actually don't really feel that well put together. You question yourself. There are those niggling doubts that keep you up at night.

Your insides don't match your outsides.

It's like a dirty dark secret that you can't speak about. And it feels like it haunts you at night when there's no-one else but you in your thoughts. And I get it, I know what that is. And I'm here to tell you it's OK, this is a safe space.

And perhaps it's finally time to say it out loud. Because you are not alone.

You are not the only one that doesn't feel that certain, confident, or self-assured when it comes to thinking about the finances in your business. Are you actually doing well? Is it well enough? You know you're doing okay, don't get me wrong. You have money coming in, your bank account looks healthy, but is it enough? Actually enough? Will it last? Will it stay at that level? Does it keep up with appearances?

I mean, who actually decides what's enough? Really?

Those questions wake you up in the middle of the night. What about... What if...

Are there enough savings? Do you even have enough of those? What about the rainy-day fund? And the credit card balance? Oh, the credit card balance. What do we do about THOSE? Will you ever pay them all off? Or are they going to be hanging round your neck forever?

And what's that looking like when it comes to family life? Will you have enough to support your kids, to cover what they want just as much as what they need? Will you be able to give them more of what you didn't have when you were growing up so they can live their best lives? Or what if you don't even have a family but the fear is real when you think about how you'll manage. How will that even work?

Then flash forward...What if you don't have enough to retire? Will you ever have enough to do that? When do you even want to retire? Where will you be by then? What does that even look like? What if all the work dries up? What if that client doesn't pay? Have they actually paid yet? Will there be any more clients?

The list goes on and you are going round and round in circles, wondering if actually all this success is enough to keep you safe in the long term.

See, you may have all this money coming in and deep down, somewhere, you know you definitely have enough. You check your banking app. Look, that's a nice balance. A healthy balance. Isn't it? But how much of it is yours? And how much belongs to the taxman? The bloody taxman.

But you need to keep your head high, you can't tell anyone about any of this, because then everyone will be able to see through you and see you for the imposter that you are. They won't understand, why would they? Because actually, they're watching you from the outside and want a bit of what they see that you have and what if that's what is keeping you rising? So, you sit with those feelings to yourself instead. Alone, and you let them fester.

You know it's got to change, but where are you supposed to turn for that reassurance anyway, especially when no-one can know.

Who is there to help you? Like you help your people? Who is going to settle your mind that, just maybe you've actually got this?

Me.

Yep, me. I'm here to tell you that you ARE doing it.

You're holding it together.

You're doing a phenomenal job.

I know it doesn't feel that way right now. You're flying by the seat of your pants. You've been feeling like that for a while. You don't confidently know how to manage your money and you know it's the key to your next level of growth. You can feel the bigger picture. It's right within arm's reach. But the certainty just isn't there. Yet.

But you make the money. You keep on making the money. It comes in, it gets you excited, but it doesn't always sit in your account for very long. And you're never 100% sure where it all goes. Is there *really* only that much left of the balance?

You see your end of year accounts prepared by your accountant. Is that a six-figure turnover figure? Yep. Yes, it is. And you did that, all by yourself. Well, that's impressive. Did you even know that's what it added up to? Were you in control of this as you went along? The bank balance is all well and good and now the tax liability is waving its flag in the air proving it, but *still*, it doesn't feel like you are in control. Are others doing better? Should it be more? How do you brush up compared to the others you look up to?

And what happens next year? Long term plans, well, those are for people more advanced in their career than you. Those are for the people who have all their ducks lined up in a nice shiny row, right? Because once you get to point B, or once you get to a turnover of X figure, or once you get to Y amount in the bank, then you can think about maybe having a family. Or expanding your family. Or maybe you can start to think about upgrading the house or moving to a 'better' area. You know, picket fence, with a tidy front garden and space in the back for the kids to run around in. Or maybe you can start putting away for the retirement fund, because what if early retirement was on the cards?

Just take a second now and indulge me, would you?

Let's just picture it for a second. Because visions become reality if we give them half a chance.

Where would that be?

What does that retirement look like? Are you near the beach? By a lake? Somewhere in the hills where you can walk for miles and literally never see another living soul? Or a townhouse in a busy city, where you're never more than a few minutes' walk from the centre of everything.

Think about this. Really think, close your eyes, and try to picture what that would look like. How does it feel? What are you wearing? What perfume do you have on? Which handbag have you got on your shoulder? What car keys do you have in your hand? Really visualise what you can see, smell, and feel. What is happening in the background, what can you hear, and touch even. Exactly what does it feel like to you?

Remember that. Write it down. Journal around it. Embrace it. Because this is the start of the plan. This is where the seed starts to grow and the roots form. This is what it's all about for you. Your North Star. The guiding light giving you more of a reason than just making money, but planning a future.

Because without forward planning, you'll never feel in control. Your spending isn't always considered, why would it be? And it's rarely ever thought through properly. What really is the best use of your money? Is now really the right time to make that investment in yourself, or are you acting on shiny object syndrome? Is it really what you need to convert the garage into a home office? Is it better to wait a bit longer, maybe delay having the hot tub installed and see what happens in the next few months?

But then you might miss your chance, right? It might never present itself again. At least not at the same rate. Because we need to be thinking past the situation now. In this moment. How do the impulsive reactions now really affect the future you desire? Should you wait, or make the jump? Take that leap of faith now? I bet your head feels like it's going to explode right about now, doesn't it? Mine is hurting for you.

But if it sounds familiar, if you can relate to any of this, then perhaps it's time to think about it a bit deeper and this is what Your Financial Flight Plan is all about.

Because I understand more than you know; I might be in the finance world, but this feels familiar to me too. Because I've been there. I'm still there sometimes; self-doubt can be absolutely crippling, but when you work for yourself and run your own business, this is all part of the game. Will those feelings and creeping thoughts ever go away? Probably not, but you're human, right? Just another story, another day.

I'm sorry, where are my manners. Please allow me to introduce myself.

My name is Tanya, and I'm the Financial Wingwoman. Let me tell you a bit about me.

I qualified as a Chartered Certified accountant in 2004, and I've been working in accountancy practice and financial training since I left school after completing my A-levels at aged eighteen. I have to boast here for a second; I absolutely love what I do.

Let me say that again. I absolutely love what I do; the clients I work with, the transformation I can offer, the satisfaction of seeing that light bulb moment, and the penny drop when that absolute understanding and realisation of "it can be the way I want it" in my clients' eyes, is the reason I do what I do.

In this book, I'm going to share with you exactly how I help my clients get to the point where the penny drops for them. I'll show you the important parts that you really can't afford to delegate to someone else, and I'll explain how you can take back that control for yourself, regardless of where you are in your journey. Because we should be in control.

I'm going to show you the detail of my trademarked MATHS® system and walk you through each of the parts of it, step by step. But most importantly, I'm going to show you how you can apply it to your business, and how it really helped me with mine.

You see, my background and experience in accountancy doesn't define me, and what I have to offer. Over the years, I've helped clients turn around failing businesses that were struggling with cash flow. I've also seen businesses expand at rapid rates and then sadly implode from the lack of support and not having the right foundations in place. I've heard the stories of business owners that have been flying high, but then hit a wall when there's a global financial crisis and suddenly those mortgage repayments are too hot to handle and they have to sell their family home. Or worse, have it repossessed. I've seen it all, and then some. I've been listened to, I've been ignored, but I've learned a whole lot in these last 25 years!

I've become a bit of a hybrid too; accountant, business mentor, financial coach, strategist, shoulder to cry on, a general mop-up-and-prop-up support system. Which is where my name comes from; I am The Financial Wingwoman, and it encompasses all of what I do and all that I can be for you. I'm in your corner, and you've got all of me and my wisdom in this book to carry with you into your future. Think of it as your little book of superpowers.

My mission is to empower people like you to take back control of your money and finances. I want to show you that what you want is more than achievable, you just don't know how to get there. You know where you want to be in life, but you're afraid that the house of cards will collapse if you do even the slightest thing different to what you're doing right now because right now, it's all you know. And it's all you've been taught when it comes to managing your finances.

Because it can feel safe.

It can be comfortable.

Even if right now it feels uncertain for you. And maybe that's showing up in different ways, maybe even physical discomfort, if you're being totally honest with yourself. But at least you know now, right? Better the devil you know, as the famous Kylie song goes.

But it doesn't have to feel this way. You can have that certainty, and that plan, and be that person that you sniff at on the outside, because deep down you're envious of the financial plans they have and the forecasts they've got in the locker. They know how much longer they'll be working for, and they know when they'll pay the mortgage off. They've got it all.

Well together, you and I can define what that ultimate success looks like for you and create the perfect flight plan to actually make it happen. And that's about to start in this little book. That journey to your North Star.

And you know what? I bet we can do it sooner than you think. I bet you'll get there quicker than you thought possible. You'll build momentum and see the results, and realise that you had the power all along. Because you actually can do it. You don't need to check in with your other half, or your parent, or other family member.

You don't need validation. From anyone.

It's all you.

And yes, you might need to check in with your accountant or finance manager, but actually have some faith in yourself that you know the questions to ask now. You know what's important in your business - the key numbers to keep an eye on, and you know the timescales you're working towards. You know how much you need to bring in to cover all your costs AND still take home what you need.

This is all possible.

You can feel like that overnight success that you see so often with the people you're surrounded by. But remember they're probably going through this too. You'd be surprised just how many people actually don't have it all together, in reality. On the outside, just like you, they look like they do. But they have the same worries, insecurities, and financial dirty secrets that they won't let see the light of day either.

You need a plan in place.

Because once you have it, and you see yourself making progress and taking one small step closer each time you check in on it, that certainty will come. The confidence will flow. And you'll be booking that cheeky extra holiday, and still be on track to where you want to be.

You can book that personal shopping experience, buy yourself some nice, classic capsule pieces for your wardrobe that match how you feel on the inside when you're bossing it in your business. You can spring for private school fees for the kids (and get to take advantage of doing it tax efficiently!), and it won't derail your long-term plans of retiring or selling your business when you want to.

Because you know now. You have the knowledge at your fingertips. You can make those considered decisions, and feel safe in doing them. And the extra three years it might take to get you where you are aiming for is a time frame you're happy with because you can see it's possible. And every decision is an informed decision that you've taken control of. You've taken back your power. It's worth the work now - a valuable trade-off - and it's more important than upping sticks and moving to the Lake District that tiny bit sooner. Because in the grand scheme of things, it's going to give you the freedom to feel back in control.

How would it feel to know that? To KNOW, and have that certainty that you've made the right decision. That it will all work out in the end because you're already walking on that path. Taking the steps. You're passing green lights on your journey, and everything is moving the way you want it to. It feels effortless. Because you have that confidence and knowledge that you know what to do. You have faith. And an absolute belief that you'll do it.

I know you can do it. I know you can because I did it too. I've been there and got several t-shirts along the way. Trust me. I know how it feels to not be in control. I know how it feels to be trapped in a situation and not have the first clue how you can turn things around. And I know the shame of not wanting to tell anyone.

Because having a flight plan is about knowing that you have everything you need in place; it's just something that you have and part of the fabric of your business. Not something you can necessarily see, like all the stitching or the care label on your favourite pair of jeans, but it's there all the same, holding everything together.

I'm not preaching.

From the outside, it probably looks like I have it all down too – even to some of those people that are closest to me. And you'd think, doing what I do, that it's always been that way. But the reason I've written this book is so that I can explain to you, all of you, what is important when it comes to managing your own business finances and what can be left to the professionals to advise you on. Because you don't need to have a finance degree or accountancy qualification to understand the important numbers of your business, to make the right financial decisions. I'll talk to you about how to screw your head on right and get all the foundations of your business in place before you feel as though you can take your training wheels off.

You can breathe now, because the biggest bit of hope I'm going to give you here is that the steps to financial independence start with delving deeper into some of the foundations you already have in place. Areas of your life, and your business, which have nothing to do with the money and are more about making good use of all the resources you currently have available.

And that's where my MATHS® system comes in.

So, I'll share my story, not for sympathy but to show you that I really do know what I'm talking about. Because I've been there myself. I won't just preach from a text book or from behind a paper certificate. I've actually got my hands dirty, turning a bad situation around that I thought I'd never get out of, to now earning a really healthy six figures in my business, and it's time I open up and share that wisdom with you.

I've carried the shame. The guilt of knowing that I really should have known better; I'm a qualified accountant, for goodness sake! I studied and learned how to do things the right way. But when I needed it the most, I still managed to get myself in a right financial pickle. I got into a mountain of debt that felt so monumentally huge that I had no possible way of paying it back and getting back on track, even though I had all the knowledge and skills to fight through it.

The weight of this was massive for me. What if people judged me? I've felt the same feelings that you do as the successful entrepreneur you are. People are looking up to you, so it's no wonder you can't tell anyone. Can't share that burden. I can still hear the imagined comments now that were spinning round in my head.

"How on earth has she managed to get in that much of a mess as an accountant?"

"How can she possibly advise me about my business and money management when she can't manage her own?"

"How can I trust her to manage my finances when she's made such a mess of her own?"

I had no-one. I had nowhere to turn. No rich parents or uncle somewhere to bail me out of the mess I'd gotten in.

Do you know how I got stuck like that? Because I'm human. Because we all make mistakes. Because we make decisions in the moment, based on emotions, on feelings, on all kinds of limiting beliefs, in circumstances we find ourselves in and conditioning that we think is factual, when actually it isn't.

I know now that it wasn't my fault. I'm not assigning blame anywhere else either, by the way, it was what it was. But the point I want to make to you is that wherever you are right now, it's not your fault either. It's not your fault you feel out of control. It's not your fault if you too have debt. It's not your fault if you spend your money and have no real plan for the future.

But we do have the power to change it now. We can take control and know that everything else will fall into place. Wherever we are financially, however we feel, it doesn't define who we are.

Winging it with your business just isn't an option anymore.

Making it up as you go along without getting the foundations in place, or just ignoring that part entirely? I get it. But it's got to stop.

Focusing on what you do best because you enjoy that part the most, and sorting the financial admin out at the weekend, or when you get a 'quiet week' (which never actually comes, does it? Let's be honest!). I hear you.

But it's those feelings that are keeping you where you are now. The uncertainty, the fear of stepping forward and upping your game because you can't face adding more uncertainty right now. You might not feel in control at the moment, but at least you will know what you are doing now feels safe.

You don't have to settle.

I want you to believe your financial dreams are achievable because they absolutely are! More than achievable, and with bells on!

Financial goals aren't just for the elite, or those brought up from upper- and middle-class backgrounds, or university educated people. And, by the way, you can be all those things, and have that background to support you, and still not have it all together.

Maybe this is the reason people feel intimidated or too scared to ask for help. Often, it's the people that come to me that look like they have it all that are the ones that need it the most. People make assumptions of others, based on preconceived ideas and it's that ego that gets in the way of stopping people from asking for the help they need when they really need it the most. That fear of not 'looking' as though they have it all together is enough to keep people stuck.

"What will people think if I don't know what questions to ask?"

"What will my accountant think if I finally say, after working with them for three years, I don't actually know what that means, can you spell it out for me again?"

"I've gone this long nodding like I know what they're talking about, I can't possibly put my hand up now and admit that what they've said for the last year has gone totally over my head"

But I'm here to tell you that this is achievable for anyone with an attitude of 'why not' instead of 'it won't work for me.'

I promise you that at least some of what I'll tell you in this book, you will already know. You may actually surprise yourself with how much you do know, but didn't realise that was all it took to have financial control. Didn't realise it would be that simple or something you could do. The groundwork for the finances isn't all about the money and it's not rocket science. As with most things, you need a framework, you need to know which bits to pull together, and you need the confidence that what you're looking at is right for you.

Sounds easy, right?

And it is... Because you rock at what you do. You just don't have a qualification in finances, and that's not your zone of genius. But we can't be great at everything. You can't be all the things to all the people.

So, whatever your circumstance, there will be no judgment from me. Only practical tools to get you from where you are now to where you want to be in the fastest time possible, without compromising on the lifestyle you currently lead.

Financial foundations are key to have in place for your business. And now is the time to learn about it. Or at least admit that you started running your business before you had these things in place and that it's okay. Because it's not about the past. It's what you do now that counts. As my grandma used to say to me, "you have to walk before you can run."

You can do it now. It's not too late, it's never too late. I've got you. You can do it for your own financial well-being and your own financial independence. You owe it to you to have that. You owe it to your kids, or your future kids if that's part of your path, because the ripple effect you create today will pass down to them too.

We're not talking trust funds, or setting them up for an easy life. I'm talking about practical tools, an actual toolkit to serve them well, that you will use and show them how it's done, and they will just see that this is the way it is when it comes to dealing with your finances.

"This is what my Mum did." How nice will that feel? Because you'll make it look easy, and you'll make them never question why they are doing it, because why wouldn't you? It's what everyone does, isn't it?

It's time to be that inspiration and make those changes. Just take my hand and follow me.

You may not want to admit the money troubles, the worries, or the fact that you need help because in this day and age, it can feel like it's more important to look like you have it all, and have it all together. But we can have help and still be the help.

Think about that plan though, the one I mentioned at the beginning. Your North Star.

It's time we roll up our sleeves and get stuck in together.

2

MY STORY

The purpose of this book is for you to see you are not alone. For you to feel safe, held, understood. Because to make the most of any financial service, accountant, or adviser you need to be able to trust them. Really trust them.

And to do that, it has to feel mutual. As I'm sitting here typing these pages, anxious about who might read them and what they might think of me, I'm deciding to be completely honest with you. I'm putting on my big girl pants and I'm going to trust you with my story, because none of us are perfect. We don't all have it all together and I really believe that for anyone that you work with in a financial capacity, you should know there is no judgement and only space for complete trust.

Now, of course, I'm not saying don't do your due diligence. Ask for recommendations, look at their testimonials. Find out what others think of their processes and manner. But how you feel about them is really important too.

Because you need to be able to open up. Tell them things you wouldn't dream about telling other people. Tell them about your hopes and dreams, your earnings, your debts, tell them everything. Speak about the inheritance you might or might not get, the divorce settlement you might be fighting tooth and nail for that's sitting over your head. You need to tell them about your fears for the joint custody battle you're knee-deep in. All the things that feel they are taking over, making you feel like you are no longer in control. Because if you don't share all the information that's important to you, you'll never get the bespoke advice in return that you truly need and deserve.

If making time for your family and being there for your youngest's sports day is at the top of your priority list, you might have your ambitious skates packed away in a drawer for now.

If your plan is to grow and sustain your business to bring your kids into the fold years from now, the advice to grow as aggressively as you can to groom the company for selling to the highest bidder in the next 18 months isn't going to be relevant for you.

So, to get the best advice and most tailored plan for your goals, you need to be prepared to get personal. You need to literally open up your underwear drawer and shine a light on everything in there; shall we take a look now?

OK, so we all know about the everyday comfy undies. The ones you may not be showing off but that you wear all the time, because they go with pretty much everything. You know, the black ones, with the lace trim? Still a bit sexy, we are not talking Bridget Jones here, but they're practical. Comfy. And these little, short numbers, represent the regular finance things that just happen. The day to day running. The things keeping you afloat.

Paying the mortgage or the rent, putting fuel in the car, paying the utility bills. We've all got those.

Then there's the greying pair, shoved at the back. Just exactly what colour are they? Is that elastic hanging out of the side? They've seen better days, and we all know those are the ones you're ashamed of; they represent the debt you can't seem to pay down, the money side of life that you'd rather didn't show its face. And no matter how many times you try and pay more than the minimum payment and build up a cash stash to clear it, something unexpected always comes along that needs paying for and the balance goes back up. I've clocked those too, I've got you.

And then, well then, phwoarrr, there's the best pair! I am HERE for these undies; these are the undies of dreams!!! You know the ones you put on that just make you feel INCREDIBLE? They make you feel done up, put together and like the true badass that you are. You feel unstoppable in those undies, before you've even put the rest of your clothes on. And these bad boys represent your goals, what you'd like to achieve, if you just dared to try. You don't wear them so often, do you? You save them for best, right? Well, let me tell you, by the end of this book, I want you to be wearing those pants all of the time.

Listen, I know, I know, this is not something you expect to talk about with an accountant. I don't prance around showcasing my knickers as a rule either. I mean you don't show that stuff to just anyone. You have to be completely at ease before any old person is seeing your grey grotties.

And that's why, right now, I'm going to open my knicker drawer. I'm going to show you that it doesn't matter what your starting point is in this game, or what baggage you carry with you. Or whether those grey pants have been sitting there forever. I'm going to tell you how I got to where I am now and you'll be able to see that, actually, despite being a qualified professional, I got completely stuck in a financial situation that I felt there was no way out of. Trapped, ashamed, what-the-hell-am-I-supposed-to-do-now, stuck. Because it happens to us all, to varying degrees, and because, well, I'm human too.

I saw with my own eyes how powerful money could be, the energy it held, the way it can affect relationships, forget friendships, be used as protection or as a weapon. See, money isn't always used in a good way.

I watched money being used to control and exploit.

I watched money being used to bully and make people feel not worthy.

I watched money be used in place of affection, love, and acceptance.

All from one inanimate object. Pieces of printed paper that hold so much value. Money has power, so it's no wonder there can be so many negative connotations attached to it.

Now, whilst I'm being honest, I have to tell you that I didn't grow up with a burning desire to be an accountant, or spend hours playing with an abacus in my formative years, dreaming of all the money I was going to make. You learn by example when you're small and, for me, back then, money was just a problem that needed to be dealt with because we didn't ever have enough of it.

"There's never enough money."

And those four simple words, have been such a huge part of my life. I was born in 1979 to parents who were pretty young at 17 and 18. My mum was the same age as my eldest daughter is now, so not even an adult, yet she was settled with the responsibility of being a mother. My brother came along a few short years later and there we were, our little family of four.

Growing up, there was never much money. My dad worked in a local Royal Mail sorting office and my mum stayed at home with us little ones. We had one of those "make do" attitudes. You've got to deal with what you are dealt, right? My Grandma often said, "made do and mended." We had hand knitted balaclavas to walk to school in and homemade jumpers for the winter. I'm not complaining, at all. It was just the way it was, and I never knew any different, you don't, do you, at that age? This was our normal.

But things took a bit of a turning point, from just getting by to struggling to make ends meet. From what I want to believe was a place of sheer desperation and a deep-seated need to support, my father was caught and convicted of theft. I don't remember exactly how old I was, but I remember being in primary school at the time and it being my first experience noticing that our lack of money made us different. Of course, I knew stealing was bad, but because of my dad's actions, I was now being tarnished by a brush that I had no control over or responsibility for. And as we know, kids can be so cruel. We lived really close to the police headquarters, so half of the kids at my school had parents who were police officers, so they all knew what my dad had done. Of course, their parents would have talked about it at home. So, as

Dad went to prison, I was singled out, an easy target for bullying when you've got a dad who's a thief. And no-one seemed to care.

So, the "I'm not worthy" grew and grew. Of course it did.

I was desperate to get away from the story of my past, of constantly being belittled and picked on. When it came to secondary school, I didn't want to move on with my classmates. I needed a change. Something different. Somewhere where people didn't know me.

Going to a private secondary school was a huge eye-opener though. I was the small fish in a very big pond and I felt insignificant, like I was not seen. I didn't have the same upbringing and it really showed. The scholarship may have gotten me in, but it was the extra things that everyone else's families paid for that I couldn't do. Like the weekend sports activities, which wasn't an option. That would mean putting more fuel in the car, which we couldn't afford. The fancy skiing trips to Switzerland with the posh outfits and latest ski mask weren't an option either, because, well, "d'ya think I'm made 'o money?" was a common statement in my house.

So, I stood out again. And in my mind, I may as well have had a giant beacon on my head saying, "look at the poor girl." Don't get me wrong, I made friends. Great friends, friends I'm still in touch with now, but the overriding effect on me was that, once again, I was an easy target for the mean girls on the playground. Except this time, it was because of my market stall clothes and cheap, cruddy shoes.

All because once again, we didn't have…you guessed it: money!

Now, let's pause for a second here. How would a situation from the past, a situation that really wasn't even of my doing, but more of a judgement from the opinions of others, based on some mistakes and a lack of funds, create a problem in my life? Surely we get over that. Surely that wouldn't affect us as adults. Well, it can. It can impact you hugely and THIS is the power of your money story. You carry it with you, just as you do those grey, grotty knickers. But when you've got those feelings of "am I bringing in enough money?," this is where the feeling comes from. Logically, you know deep down that of course you are, but you can't stop thinking it. That creeping doubt. When this happens, yes, that past is sitting there haunting you.

And when you actually work back through it, and remember how those situations felt to you at the time, you can completely see why. Because your brain stores those memories and feelings and they form a part of who you are. Like a core memory in Disney's Inside Out. Have you seen that movie? (Great movie!) They don't get lost in the depths of your long-term memory bank, they affect who you become and how you respond and react to events later in life. It's your brain's way of trying to keep you safe. To always remember what could go wrong, what could happen. It wants you to subconsciously remember them so it never happens again. Even if what happened isn't even a result of something you did, or the reality now.

But of course, as we all do in life, we get through it, don't we? Those turbulent teenage years are tough for everyone, but we have to see them as the grit that makes us who we are. I realised really quickly that although I had a disadvantaged start, compared to others, I didn't have to stay there. I could make something of myself. I could change the narrative, if I chose to work at it.

So, I got my head down, got some decent grades, with the intention of going to university. I wanted that. But the old money monster reared its head again because who was I to go to university? It's expensive, my parents wouldn't be able to afford it, and that assumption meant I didn't even ask. So, goodbye seriously cool dreams of studying biochemistry, and hello reality: Serious debt and 'no good with money.'

You are going to have to think of something else Tanya because "money brings nothing but problems."

Life was turbulent. Mum and Dad had split and Dad took the little money we had with him, so, if we were struggling before, now it was turbulent. With limited funds and limited supplies, the times were scary and uncertain. I was still at home; it was all I'd ever known. But I had to contribute financially. Mum hadn't worked for 17 years. So now she's got a 17-year-old and a 14-year-old and no way of earning more than what the state would provide. She was awarded £2.50 per week in child maintenance, per child, which was a real smack in the face.

And I was angry.

Where was my dad in all of this? He could have helped, financially. And sometimes he would, but there would always be a string attached to it. A price that needed to be paid to get what we needed as a family. It was like he used money as a weapon to get what he wanted. It always had to work for him first.

"I'll never be in that place where you are now."

My mum somehow managed to get us through, after all, things always work out in the end. Do you know that feeling of this too shall pass? I'm not sure specifically where the inner rebel in me was born, but I distinctly remember looking at my mum one evening, in a helpless puddle on the floor. She didn't know how the mortgage was going to get paid the following week and was facing the prospect of another week on the cheery 4p beans to feed us all.

And I couldn't help but to say to myself "I'll never be in that place where you are now." And I wasn't even looking down at her. I guess, in a way, I'd admired how much she'd managed to achieve once everything was taken away from her. But I was never, ever going to leave myself in a position where I was dependent on someone else financially. I wanted to be in absolute control of my own money at all times. I needed a job. I had no idea what job, I didn't have a career plan, but I needed to take action. I felt that fire within me.

So, I may not have known what or where, but I felt confident that this was the right route. Unfortunately, others didn't quite feel the same. I still remember the look on my form tutor's face when I told her I wasn't filling in the university applications they kept forcing under my nose. You'd think I'd said I was going to burn the school down. But those forms weren't about me. It was about the school's reputation and the statistics and tick boxes that needed ticking.

I was adamant though; in full-on rebel mode, I started skipping registration and dodging the staff in corridors, a-la James Bond style. I was getting a job, so I applied for the only job advert on the school careers noticeboard at the time, which for an apprenticeship accountant position in Blackpool. That shut them up and got them off my back.

I didn't think I'd actually get the position.

Especially with those voices in my head saying I wasn't good enough and I wouldn't amount to anything, but apparently, my luck had started to change. I was offered the job on the spot. Maybe I did have prospects, opportunities, and a glimpse at a future after all. I didn't need to get into debt or go to university, I could learn and earn at the same time. Winner. It was the perfect solution. I was ready to start the next chapter of my life.

But it wasn't over.

Oh no! That would be easy. Within days of turning eighteen, I was seduced by the credit card applications dropping onto the doormat. 'Free' money. Well, that was incredibly alluring for me. I could finally buy a suit from a department store instead of what my mum had managed to find for me in the local end-of-line stock warehouses. I had 'money' in my purse for the first time in my life. And I could worry about paying it back later.

I met someone and later fell in love. I was seduced again, but this time by someone of the other sex and I truly fell hook, line, and sinker. He was charming, affluent (apparently), and so beyond anything I believed I could possibly measure up to. I was completely infatuated. Putty in his hands. But he saw me coming.

He'd say things like "people are only nice to me because of my money." What if he thought that of me? So, I went out of my way to prove this wasn't the case. I would insist on paying for my share of everything. I would buy him gifts I couldn't afford, pay for meals out, I would repay him for anything that he paid for on my behalf at break-neck speed. But that debt was racking up and I didn't dare tell him about it. I kept that secret all to myself. I believed I had to compete financially to be worthy in a relationship. I was overspending daily.

But, as with a lot of debt, it got gradually worse. I couldn't survive financially each month without using my credit cards. He'd cottoned on to it and used it as a stick to beat me with, insinuating I was only with him for his money, because I was so bad at managing my own. I'd proved him right. And it left me feeling down-trodden, lonely and miles away from the people who loved me. I had nothing. So, despite being desperately unhappy, I stuck it out. I'd become my mum but with a credit card rather than a person to rely on.

Let's also not forget the profession I was working in. Mismanaging my own personal finances does not mix well with being taken seriously in the accountancy and financial training fields! The shame of this was crippling, and only continued to feed into my feelings of not-enoughness and the constant self-blame I buried myself under.

Fast forward a few years and I was using one credit card to make the minimum payment on another. I was living on my credit cards and overdraft as well as limited maternity pay for my first child and it didn't cover half of what I was committed to financially on a monthly basis. My other half made it very clear that the responsibility of raising a baby was all mine. He used this time to work longer hours, to be away more on the weekends. He was hardly ever at home, so I had no respite and I couldn't afford to pay a babysitter to take a few hours off.

I was so busy blaming myself for my situation, that it took me several years to realise I was in a financially controlling relationship.

I wasn't allowed to see my friends after work, because he couldn't or wouldn't care for our child. He wouldn't take her to nursery in the mornings because he "couldn't bear to say goodbye to her." I wasn't 'allowed' to wear high heels. I was too overweight. I couldn't visit my family because he didn't want me to take our baby away from him for a few days. I couldn't win.

The iron bars of the cage I was in were firmly closing in. I had no means to be able to leave. This was my life now.

But the fight is real.

I don't know where my inner rebel came from or how she was still going, but I knew I deserved more. I didn't deserve to feel helpless, trapped as a 21st century Cinderella. The light of my life, my little girl, was five now, and about to start school. I was close to £30,000 in personal debt and I needed to start clearing it to better our lives. But I'd got a great job, with a hefty pay rise, and I could finally get things like a nanny for our little human. I wasn't alone.

Eventually, I woke up. A throwaway comment that went something along the lines of "Well, I've got to put up with you now, like you've got to put up with me" really was the straw that broke the camel's back. My rebel rose and she bellowed in my head "Really? I don't think so."

So, whilst I made all my plans under the surface, I remained in the house we had bought together, but we lived very separate lives. The plus side of having a five-bedroom house did mean that there was plenty of space for me to move into a room of my own, with an en-suite bathroom, and with space for a little desk in the corner.

Exactly seven years later, my life had completely turned around again. I paused to take stock of my financial situation. And, for the first time in my adult life, I had zero debt. I realised, it didn't have to be the way it had always been and I had a choice. A choice to be different. A choice to change things. A choice to live how I wanted to live.

But I'm glad all these things have happened. I think they've brought me to where I am today. And I am still debt free, save for the mortgage on the dream house I live in with my new husband and two girls. I have two thriving businesses that make a great profit, and I have savings and investments behind me to provide that financial security, even if there are times when it feels harder.

I've found what I've been searching for my whole life.

So, all the limiting beliefs, the comments I'd never dream of saying to anyone else but I'd say them in my own head, weren't true. It turns out that I was able to achieve everything I'd ever wanted. But I needed to really look within myself to do it. To not blend in. To not settle. But to believe that there was always another way.

The birth of The Financial Wingwoman is about showing women that we can reclaim our power and take back control, regardless of our story and our circumstance. Regardless of feeling marginalised, or 'not being any good with numbers' or not feeling worthy of what we desire.

Because if I can, then you can too.

I didn't tell you my story for sympathy. I wanted to show you that it doesn't matter what your background is, what has happened in the past or your lack of knowledge in certain areas. Even if you 'should' know better, or you've had the benefit of a prestigious education, it doesn't define who you are and it doesn't need to hold you back now. They're just lessons. Lessons that form what we do next. What we change. And we can say thank you for those.

It doesn't matter what your starting point is. I'm going to show you the steps that I took to turn my life around and show you how you can replicate that, but here's the truth; there is no magic key for this. You actually need to do the work.

There are no pre-qualifying conditions or selective upbringings that mean you aren't able to access how to do this. You don't need a private education, you don't need a finance qualification, you don't need to be married to a millionaire; you have totally got this! The only person stopping you from doing this is you.

Why do we stop ourselves?

There are two main reasons for this: fear and a lack of knowledge.

We tackle fear by facing the bullies and our own demons; by opening that brown envelope and by reading our bank statements. By being honest with ourselves and facing the thing we've been avoiding.

The bottom line is that, without goals, you have no flight plan. Without a flight plan, how do you get from where you are now to where you want to be?

Once you know what you're dealing with, you can take action. Because when you know, you know! It's that simple. You can make new plans, you can change direction, or at the very least, you can ask for help and know, with confidence, you are getting what you need.

And you're in my world now. Take my knowledge into your future, and you'll have everything you need in the pages of this book, and the extra resources you'll be able to find on my website in the relevant signposted references.

Ultimately, <u>you</u> get the benefit of doing this work. You are going to take the journey, you will have the satisfaction of achieving what you set out to, and you won't even have to do it alone. I'll be right here with you.

All you have to do is get out of your prickly, uncomfortable chair that you're so used to sitting in, and go get that financial potential that you're craving and know you deserve.

3

WHAT IS THE MATHS® SYSTEM?

These next few chapters are going to include all the practical stuff that I take all my clients through. My MATHS® system has been designed as a bit of a nod to my secondary school maths teacher who told my parents that I wouldn't be able to cope with A-Level maths. Yes, even then, I was learning subconsciously from the comments around me that I was 'crap' at maths! It's also the reason that I like this name though. It's a constant reminder that I get to change the narrative. And so many people feel the same. Crap with numbers. Crap with maths. Well, let's rewire that belief.

The different components of the system are:

Mindset

Understand the power of your mindset, specifically your money mindset. I'll explain how you can overcome wherever limiting beliefs negatively impact you in business.

Accountability

Learn how to master the CEO mindset and keep yourself accountable. I'll show you how to identify your strengths and how to delegate what you no longer need to work on.

Timetabling

Get to grips with maximising the one truly non-renewable resource that is time. I'll give you the tools to maximise your earning potential and provide the most value to your clients.

Housekeeping

Make the financial non-negotiables of running your business as easy to keep on top of as possible. I'll highlight for you which are the key numbers to keep an eye on and how to plan ahead of the big stuff, like paying yourself and the tax man.

Solutions

Prioritise your own peace of mind with some hands-on guides and tools to put your own flight plan together. The sky is the limit; where will your plans take you?

MATHS! By working through each of these steps, and acknowledging how important they each are in tackling your financial foundations for yourself, you'll start to realise that dealing with the numbers in your business isn't actually that hard, and that you can do it yourself.

And, as I've said, this isn't just about the finances. Our habits and how we live our life is a reflection of how we are with our money and finances, so the MATHS® system brings in other aspects too. As with finances, we need to look at the foundations of how we behave as individuals, to shine a light on our behaviours and how they can affect us on a day-to-day basis.

Understanding how all these pieces fit together will be the first step to unlocking financial independence for yourself. It isn't just about the money, it's about all the resources you have at your disposal.

Being in control is not about being good with numbers; it comes with organisation and a belief that you're worthy of it. If you don't feel like this right now, then it's time to look at why. Your money story doesn't have to be your money future.

Let's do this, shall we?

4

MINDSET

According to the Oxford dictionary, mindset is 'a set of attitudes or fixed ideas that someone has and that are often difficult to change.'

When it comes to running your business, it's not just your own mindset, attitudes, and fixed ideas you have to focus on; it's also those of everyone else around you. This might include: your immediate and extended family and their thoughts and opinions of your success, your customers and the imprints of their own mindset onto your own, the suppliers you deal with, the business associates you work with, and so on.

Often, when we talk about money, we fear that we are being judged. So much of a business is judged on its financial success, or our understanding of the money in and money out process. How many times have you spoken to your accountant and felt like they were talking down to you? Or expect you to know all the lingo they barrage you with?

Now, are they really doing that? Talking down to you? Or have you already told yourself that you are not going to understand whatever comes out of their mouth so you've already switched off before the conversation has even started?

The absolute hardest part of all of this? Even if you just start with thinking about yourself, a lot of the time, you aren't even aware that those fixed ideas and attitudes are there in your subconscious brain all the time, influencing every thought you have and every decision you make.

All. Of. The. Time.

There's no escape from it, there's no amount of down time that will get rid of it. It gives you that unexplainable nervous feeling in the pit of your stomach, it affects your energy levels and the quality of your sleep. It can even put you off your food, or make you go the other way and reach for foods or drink out of comfort that you wouldn't normally indulge in.

This is mindset. So, it's no wonder Mr. Dictionary is saying it's difficult to change.

Our brain uses our subconscious and unconscious parts to protect you. To keep you safe. It affects your emotions and forms part of your instincts that you use to survive. It's your built-in survival skills that have been learnt from all the lessons along the way. From even before you, if you can believe that.

In prehistoric times, this instinctual part would have served you well when a sabre-toothed tiger stumbled into your cave and you needed to run, or you happened upon a Triceratops and you had to climb a tree at break-neck speed.

But we are not in prehistoric times, we don't need quite the same level of survival skills. Yet for some reason, we still feel the need to act like the Alpha in our own lives. We don't have to act in these fight or flight responses. But we do, however, have a very active emotional brain, which is the limbic part. It's responsible for how we feel about things, and how we react to certain situations, without conscious thought.

The key word there is <u>react</u>. When left unchallenged, our emotional brain can very easily take over from our logical brain when we drop too much into how things feel, instead of thinking rationally about our dilemma or circumstances.

Let's say, for example, someone commented something nasty on your recent social media post and it hurt your feelings. You might instantly question your professional ability, your whole zone of genius and the reason you're in business at all. This leads to wanting to hide and you doubt that you can ever show your face in online circles, ever again. You have been judged. Your authority questioned. You feel crushed, in that split moment.

What does your emotional brain do? It wants to make you feel better. So, it searches your memory bank and in the blink of an eye it reminds you of what you like to do, the instant gratification things that flood your body with feel-good hormones to make you feel good again.

What is that for you? A glass of wine? Ordering a takeaway? Heading to the gym to lift some iron? A spot of online shopping on your phone to buy yourself some essential gadgets that will not only give you that instant feel-good hit, but will undoubtedly improve your business, increase your efficiency as well as your ability to multi-task, all in one fell swoop! Yep, this is our emotional brain going "there, there, buy yourself something pretty."

And then, at some point over the course of the evening, or maybe by the next morning, your neocortex kicks in and the logical, more rational, thinking part of the brain is back in control. You read that social media comment back again, and you realise that you perhaps misread it initially. Perhaps you've overreacted, it doesn't come across quite so scathing as you initially received it on your first read through yesterday.

You can see now how it might have been intended to be read. And it's actually quite interesting, as constructive comments and feedback tend to be, if accepted in the intended way. But now you're feeling grumpy because you didn't have a great night's sleep; you're also regretting that pizza, the tub of ice cream, and the bottle of wine that you polished off last night while your emotional brain was looking out for you.

Okay, okay, maybe this is an extreme example, but this is what can very easily happen when the emotional part of our brain is allowed to take over our actions; when we react, in the moment, instead of stopping, considering all the angles, then, and only then, taking conscious action. If we could somehow train ourselves to slow down, notice the reactions for what they are, and allow space for rational thought to kick in, we might be able to teach ourselves different habits.

Because that's the problem with reactions; they become habit-forming, and then they become self-perpetuating, and when you then say it out loud in conversation with someone, it becomes more of a fact about you, rather than how you reacted in a moment to a certain situation.

Here are some examples:

I am a comfort eater

'I am', did you notice that? You can't get much more positive and firmer than using 'I am' to start a sentence.

I hate conflict

'Hate', another powerful word. We tell ourselves we hate something, and our emotional brain goes into overdrive to help us avoid feeling this way ever again. We hate that now. That's our view for now, it's not written in stone.

I am rubbish at numbers

There it is again, 'I am'. Positive, firm, powerful, not budging, a confirming statement.

Continuing to use this language over time means that you will believe what you are saying to yourself. Your brain hears 'I am' on repeat and it forms part of your identity, if you let it.

When actually, these actions, and the way we react to certain situations, don't define who we are. We are in a state of choice all the time. Just because we've walked through the door on a Friday evening, after a long and trying day, and poured ourselves a large glass of wine before we've even taken our shoes off, doesn't define how you have to feel about yourself from then on. It doesn't mean that it has to become a habit, because you choose not to let it. You hold that power.

Exercise

Let's consider expanding and questioning those statements that you tell yourself.

If we explore a little bit more around those short statements, it gives us more to work with so that we can break down the overall situation and start to see what we can change and take back some control for ourselves.

Find yourself a pen and a journal and use this simple structure to explore what's going on for you a little bit more:

"When...(something happens), I.................................(do something) because.........................(what's the reason you do this?) to..................................... (change how I'm feeling).

Be honest. Don't overthink it. Write out the first thing that comes into your head.

What triggers you to feel a certain way?

What is your go to 'vice' to feel better?

What does that provide for you?

How does it change how you feel?

As an example:

"When I feel attacked by a comment from others on social media, I reach for a chocolate biscuit because they're my favourite/convenient and I won't care so much about what's been said."

"When I make a mistake, I pour a glass of wine so that I can relax and not worry so much about it"

"When I feel overwhelmed, I scroll mindlessly through social media to lose myself in other people's posts to distract myself in something, anything, that isn't what I've got going on."

"When I feel swamped by my work commitments, I shop online, because it holds all the answers and solutions, so I can buy something that will improve my efficiency/save me time/give me something new the play with and I feel better."

Whatever those examples look like for you, there is no right or wrong answer, so remember there's no judgement here. What comes up for you? Just think about the last time you felt a certain way and let your pen write and run away with your thoughts.

Get curious; think about what you had going on at the time. Were you on your own, or with other people? Think about the feelings that you felt.

If we can explore those statements and add context to them, we can try to pinpoint what causes us to do certain things. Is it a person that brings out that reaction in you? Is it a certain topic of conversation? Try to think a little around the subject, and don't try too hard. Your brain will take you there if you relax into the exercise for a few minutes.

With a bit of exploration, we can then start to question what's actually going on, instead of believing our own statements of affirmation (which our emotional brains interpret as facts). With our logical brain, we can interrupt the norm and start to rationally question these statements.

Here are some things you could consider:

- When you've perceived that negative things have

happened to you, where are you and what are you doing at the time?

- Is it a personal situation or a work situation?
- Who are the people involved?
- Does this happen regularly?
- How are you feeling generally that day? What is your mood?
- Are you working on a particular task/client/program?
- Does it involve an emotive subject, such as money or time management?
- What feelings does it bring up for you either mentally or physically?
- What is your go to action that you would prefer not to do so impulsively?
- How does this action serve you – does it help or inflame a situation?
- Are you making this worse by having things easily to hand or in reach?
- Do specific things trigger these repeated actions?
- What could you do about it to change your habit?
- Do these actions that you go to on autopilot actually give you the satisfaction you think they will?
- Be honest here, do you actually cherish all those impulse purchases and make use of every last one?
- Do you enjoy every last bite of that pizza and not regret that feeling of bloat afterwards?
- Did that bottle of wine help you to not think about the issue you were avoiding, and solve all your perceived problems, or did it just give you a headache the next morning when you needed to face them again?

By questioning the assumptions and automatic statements that we make, we can start to break the habit patterns. By being honest with ourselves, we can build up our own inner trust radar.

TIP: You might need to do this a few times to get used to it, especially if you've never done anything like this before. It is about trusting yourself to see what comes up when you relax into thinking about certain situations, but you will start to notice patterns and you can then question each part of the sentence. And that's when you can start to take action.

Be gentle with yourself, and don't worry if your negative thoughts don't disappear straight away. Our emotional brain has done a really good job of keeping us alive as humans for the last however many thousands of years, so it is just doing what it's always done. It isn't your fault that you've allowed it to just do what it was meant to do by trying to keep us happy and safe.

With understanding and recognition that the brain is made up of different parts, we can choose which parts we tap into when we give ourselves the toolkit to access them, which will enable us to pause, think and make a different choice. It just takes a bit of practice.

Mindset is so powerful. But it's exactly that, it's in our mind, so we can implement the power of choice and can take responsibility for how we respond and actually behave. When we start to question those instinctive thoughts, and notice when our brain hints at the wine in the fridge, and realise that it won't improve anything, that's when we can take control and do things differently. We've identified the belief, we are now conscious of it, so we can change the action.

Learning how you react in business situations, and understanding how you can respond as the CEO you are meant to be, is the first step in the MATHS® process. It's a big reminder that, to make the best choices for your business, you need to step outside of the everyday habits and find ways to remove the emotion. Situations in business are often only made personal because of how we respond to them.

Making the time to work on your business, instead of continually working in your business, is how you can start to prioritise its overall direction. With this comes the clarity of what needs to happen and the changes you need to make in order to shape it to be the perfect flight vessel to get you where you want to be; at your North Star.

How do you adopt the mindset of a CEO?

To create change, you need to do something different to what you've done before. As Henry Ford famously said, " If you always do what you've always done, you'll always get what you've always got" It's time to be bolder, braver!

Give these suggestions a try if you find yourself struggling with where to start:

1. A CEO has a bigger picture plan in their mind. A short-term, medium-term and a long-term plan. For you, building a picture of what financial independence looks like for you, your starting point should be your North Star. What is your goal? What does that dream life look like? What sort of time frame would you put on reaching it? Then start to work backwards from there. If you have a plan for twenty years from now, what needs to be in

place by fifteen years from now to be on track? Then ten years from now, and so on. Each time you then make a decision, it will be an informed one and it will be with your overall vision in mind to achieve your long-term goal.

2. Formalise the time you want/need to spend on your business in your diary. Do you find yourself trying to keep time to one side, but when clients come calling, you give it up for them? Treat your own business as you would a client; it's just as important to keep you on track for what you want to achieve. Block the time out in the diary and keep it sacred.

3. Have the systems and people in place to give you the information you need to be able to make informed decisions when you need it. If this is something that you keep tight hold of yourself, for fear of losing control, sometimes we need to remember that we have to relinquish control of the small things to gain control of the bigger picture.

4. Simplify, optimise, and streamline your processes. We'll talk about this more in the Accountability chapter, but by measuring the results currently, it becomes easy to compare to and see how improvements can be made, and how successful your changes have been. You can also track how margins can be improved, and where time can be saved.

5. Accept that there is only so much you can do to manage risks. Things will go wrong sometimes and mistakes will be made. Mitigate these risks as far as is feasibly possible, with insurances and having checks in place. As long as there is learning, then there will be value in the exercise, even if it feels negative at the time.

Money mindset

Working on your money mindset is going to be one of the most powerful tools in your armour.

We've already seen the power of an affirmative statement in our brain. Take the example of 'I'm no good with money.' We don't even need to say it aloud (even though we often do!) for it to stick in our brain, and it then becomes a self-fulfilling prophecy. Our brain then shows us all the times that we have been 'no good with money' (because you ran up a balance on a credit card before you realised it) and we then see it as 'the truth' and just accept 'this is what I do' or 'this is who I am,' rather than knowing we can take back control and actually make change.

Let's take this beyond the examples we've talked about already and think about all those things you tell yourself. Those things that you've built up over years of perhaps being too hard on yourself, or feeling like an imposter, or having perfectionist tendencies. And then you add to that the emotive beast that is money.

We can't help that money has this effect on us. We're human beings after all, and we're creatures of habit, as we've already explored. Our relationship with money is dependent upon our history with it and the stories we've heard, or the feelings we've felt about it, while growing up.

Perhaps you grew up in a relatively comfortable family home, and money wasn't really something you registered as something to worry about, because it was always just there. Perhaps Mum and Dad experienced a struggle when they were growing up and were determined to give you a better start in life, and make sure you never wanted for anything. So, for you, you'd never experienced the scarcity that they came to believe was 'normal.' Instead, you grew up with everything you've ever wanted, and more to the point, you also perhaps never really appreciated or understood the value of what was being given, or the money needed to give it, and how that money was earned. So that presents its own challenges for you.

Maybe you grew up in an environment like I did and believed that money was something that caused problems and created fear, because there was never enough and you are not worthy or deserving of having any money.

All these experiences that we see in our lives, become memories. They are often stored alongside the voices that we heard at the time, the music that was playing on the radio, the tone of the conversation, the atmosphere in the room - and how we felt in any given moment. Our emotional brain then processes those feelings and links them to the statements we hear, and the things we see.

For a small person, up to the age of around 7 years old, our brains are still forming. It's like a sponge. It can't differentiate between what is fact and the whole story behind a situation, and what is a feeling.

So, for example, when someone's angry about a broken vase, the true root of the issue is often the sentimental value of the item, or that there might not be available funds to replace it. The anger isn't necessarily that an accident has happened resulting in a broken vase. However, for you as a child, you would register the broken item and how the anger made you feel. For you now, in this situation, a broken item means fear of the 'inevitable' anger that will follow.

A throwaway comment, such as *'we can't afford that, do you think money grows on trees?'* becomes fact. Money is scarce. You have to work really hard to make money. It isn't readily available, like fruit on trees.

And this can cause feelings of fear and lack, because you are not able to have what your friends have, and you then feel left out and picked on because of your parents' financial situation. All of these feelings provide you with 'proof' that these beliefs are 'fact.'

Not all money stories have to be negative. What about the happiness it brings when money is plentiful, because we have presents, and ice cream, and amazing days out, creating memories? Memories that can only be associated with being able to spend loads of money, instead of making the most of other pleasures, such as family walks, playing a board game, spending time talking to friends.

But physical money isn't emotive at all. Think about it. It's a tangible physical thing. It's a commodity. It's something we exchange for another thing of the same value. It's a resource.

Maybe that's where the problem comes from when it comes to money decisions in our businesses, as well as just dealing with money in general. It's all so complicatedly tangled up in memories and thoughts and feelings from the past, instead of being something that we can factually and rationally make decisions with right now, with our situation in the moment.

So, it's no wonder really that it's very easy to get lost in the 'value' of something, or question the 'value' of our services for our clients, so we over give to justify the cost they've spent. And that creates a knock-on effect on how much we charge our clients, or how much we provide as part of a service for our fees.

How would it feel to be able to unpick this, and be able to consciously take a step back and look at our own beliefs, habits, and stories that we tell ourselves, and actually question them and rewrite our money story?

We don't have to accept that what we've always known is our 'truth.' We have the power now to question this and determine our own version of the story. We have the power to be able to do that rationally, as an empowered adult, aware of the facts. Not a child taking in and absorbing all that is happening around them.

We get to ask:

Is it really true?

Why is it true?

Who said it's true, and do we agree?

Does it still apply to me?

Is that my belief I'm carrying or someone else's?

I want to tell you a powerful story about a bouncy ball.

It's one from my childhood, and it formed the whole basis for the work that I do now with my clients; it's the reason I trained to be a certified financial coach and it also helped me to reframe my own limiting beliefs around charging my worth, recognising the transformation I can bring for my clients, and money in general.

I would guess I would have been around 9 years old, so around the age that my youngest daughter is now. I had one or two friends that lived outside of walking distance from where we lived, without crossing a main road, so I didn't see them outside of school very often. But this one weekend, I had a playdate at a friend's house that was a good 10-minute drive away. I was excited! My mum gave me a pound coin to take with me 'just in case of an emergency.'

Got it. No problems. Thank you very much. Although she didn't actually clarify what that 'emergency' might be, but never mind, I've got the emergency pound. Safely in my pocket.

There were three of us together and we all had a great time. It was all new to me as I didn't get invited out often, thanks to the questionable choices of my father, so I was in my element, and the occasion felt quite special and important.

We went out for a short walk and popped into the 'corner shop.' I can't remember whether it was on an actual corner of the road at all, but we called all of these types of shops 'corner shops' in those days. You know the ones; the all-in-one shop! The sweet shop, the paper shop, the Post Office, the convenience store, the tobacconist, the mini-pharmacy (if a plaster and a paracetamol was all you needed) and so on.

My friends started picking up things that they were going to buy, so I did the same. I had money in my pocket, after all! And this felt pretty much like an emergency to 9-year-old me, because I didn't want to be the only one left out that didn't buy something when my friends were. They'd think I was poor.

I selected one of those big refresher sweets, the chewy ones with the sour sherbet in the middle, and a bouncy ball. Not just any bouncy ball, it was a big one, and it was awesome. I was willing to bet that it would have bounced higher than any other bouncy ball I'd ever seen. I didn't have one of these at home, and this would be all mine. I wanted it. So, I bought it with my very own in-case-of-emergency money.

I was so proud of my ball. I played with it for the rest of the afternoon, and it was bloody marvellous.

When I went home, my mum asked me if I'd had to spend the money she'd given me. I'd almost forgotten, the ball was still in my pocket. Yes, I explained chirpily. I'd bought a sweet and "look at this bouncy ball Mum, isn't it the best bouncy ball you've ever seen?" "Come outside with me a minute Mum, (no balls allowed inside, under any circumstances!) and I'll show you how high it bounces…"

But, to my disappointment, Mum didn't follow me. She stood still and asked if I had any change for her. I skipped back and dropped the 6p into her open hand. I remember this so specifically, because it was an old 5p coin and it was bigger than the 1p coin next to it, which isn't the case anymore.

My Mum just looked at the change in the palm of her hand, and quietly said to me "That's all the money I have now to last me all week," and she turned her back to me and walked away.

Now, as a parent myself, I understand what my mum was trying to do. She wanted to teach me the potential consequences of running out of money by wasting it on things you don't need. Like this glorious bouncy ball.

But that isn't the lesson I took from that experience.

I learned:

I make bad decisions when it comes to money.

When you spend money, it's gone and you don't have enough for anything else.

I can't be trusted with money.

I don't deserve to buy things for myself.

Now, to be clear, my mum didn't tell me any of these things. And she couldn't possibly have known this would be what I would carry with me from that experience, because everyone experiences things differently and individually for themselves. But that's what makes dealing with money mindset such a minefield. Because you never know what you are imprinting on someone in that exact moment. Or that you even thought it was a thing in the first place, but it's churning away in the back of your mind all the time when you are making financial decisions.

And it also makes it really hard to unpick and understand where all your instincts and the stories we tell ourselves about money come from. Do they actually relate to money at all? Or is it just about a silly little bouncy ball that we really, really wanted when we were young to keep up appearances with friends?

I never played with that ball again. I felt too guilty to even get it out of the hiding place that I kept it for a short while and eventually I threw it in the bin. I may have got rid of the ball and grown up since then, but I carried those limiting beliefs with me as though they were my truth. And I believed them too, until I was talking to a gorgeous and trusted friend of mine who questioned my throw-away comment about not deserving something. She asked me where that came from. And this memory popped up.

She helped me to understand what it meant; she helped me to understand how I had distorted the message formed in my young brain, and she showed me how it was showing up in my business today; as a stick to hit myself over the head with.

I wasn't worthy of charging a fair price for my services.

I wasn't worthy of being paid for my services.

I couldn't be trusted to make important decisions about purchasing for my business or myself.

I wasn't worthy of being paid back money that I'd lent to someone.

Now, as part of my work as a financial coach, I understand even more about this. I understand how it impacts my thoughts and actions, and also how it can be changed. As with everything I've talked about in this chapter, we can choose what we believe, and it's really important that you remember that. I'll say it again.

You have the power to choose what you believe.

You can build your own truth with new experiences if you're brave enough to challenge your old beliefs. But first, we have to know what the old beliefs are.

And now? Well now, I can also rewrite those affirmations for myself, which is exactly what I did, along with going straight online (a totally non-emotional purchase, in case you were wondering!) and ordered myself a new bouncy ball! This one is pink; it sits on my desk and makes me happy. I deserve the bouncy ball. It doesn't have that hold over me anymore. It's a reminder that I changed the narrative.

My services are valuable and I can charge my worth.

I deserve to be paid for the services I provide.

I make good decisions with money for my business and myself.

I deserve to be repaid for money loaned to others within the agreed terms.

Exercise

Similar to the earlier exercise in this chapter, I want you to think about your money story, and all the things you tell yourself about money. Why you can't earn it, why you can't keep it, why you overspend it, or whichever scenario applies to you.

- Where do your thoughts around money hold you back?
- What obstacles do you have around money in your business?
- Do you find yourself delaying sending invoices after completing work?
- Are you comfortable talking about your prices with your clients?

Then, if you're feeling brave, write yourself a timeline of your money story, starting with your earliest money memory that you can remember right up to significant memories to date.

Which people were involved?

How did it feel for you?

What happened?

Use the suggested prompts from earlier in this chapter, if it helps, and journal around these. Watch out for those negative statements of limiting belief and think about how you could reframe them, just as I've done from my bouncy ball lesson.

Now, this isn't a one-off exercise, and it starts with awareness. Once you're aware of the impact that your subconscious limiting beliefs have on all areas of your life, you can notice the thoughts in your head, where these impact you in your life and when you perhaps hold yourself back.

Remember, you don't have to do what you've always done, no matter how alien or uncomfortable it might feel to start with.

The next time you notice your immediate thoughts in your head, just take a second to acknowledge them. Shine some light and awareness on them, and question them.

Is it true?

Is it your belief?

Whose belief is it?

Where did it come from?

When did you first hear it?

How does it make you feel?

Do you remember feeling that same way at other times?

What's the connection to how you feel now?

Let's go back to that definition at the start of this chapter. The one that stated that mindset is a set of fixed ideas that are often difficult to change. Well, what did the Oxford dictionary know, anyway? Now you know how to change those mindset cobwebs hanging in your closet.

Remember, the aim here isn't to fix everything in one fell swoop. The aim here is awareness. And curiosity.

Any weakness, worry, perceived or apparent failing, while you're being hard on yourself, isn't actually a failing or disaster at all.

None of it is your fault. You have dived into your business and have done awesomely well with your skill set. You just didn't realise your brain was trying to sabotage you while trying to keep you safe. But it's okay now, you can tell your brain you've got this.

Acknowledging this now, and noticing when things come up for you, is the first step. Don't forget that you can never know what you don't know. It's time to forgive yourself for some of the things you are frustrated with yourself for. It's all something that can be changed, when you choose to believe you can overcome it.

Mindset is probably the biggest part of the puzzle, and perhaps the one that will take the longest for you to work through. Not because it's difficult as such, but because you'll unearth new things all the time. Like peeling an onion, as you work through one issue and remove a layer that's holding you back, you'll find another layer underneath. I'm still discovering things about my money story, and it's something that is worth continuing to invest in for yourself, time wise.

5

ACCOUNTABILITY

So, how's that mindset looking? And how are you now feeling about rolling up your sleeves, getting down and dirty and really honest about what it is you truly want from your business? Because as business owners, it's not just enough to know the short-term goals or the next move you are going to make. We have to dig a little deeper. To truly understand what we are really doing it for. You know, that reason that fuels you and wakes you up in the middle of the night because you can't stop thinking about it; that gets you excited when you sit still for a second and imagine that you've already got there and the plan is set.

And remember, however that looks for you, nothing is right or wrong. This is your journey and what you want your business to look like and why you do it is completely down to you. But don't panic if you haven't dared to think about it, if that feels a little too big. What happens if you take the pressure off and just ask yourself what do you desire, here and now? Why not give it a go? Create your business vision board. Cut things out of magazines, picture that life you want and put it somewhere prominent so that you can be reminded of those epic goals on a regular basis.

The only thing that is stopping you from then achieving that vision is you. You might not have the tools yet, but you've got the vision. So, once you know what you need to do, you've got to believe it too. And then you're half way there. Woah, living on a prayer!

So, it's time to get practical. You've got the plan. You know the path. So, what's stopping you?

Is it that you don't know how? That's okay, we'll cover that in our Housekeeping and Solutions chapters.

You don't have time? The Mindset chapter should help you with this because that's a limiting belief right there. You get to make the time. Time for you and your business. Plus, the Timetabling chapter will give you practical tips to start taking action.

Maybe you're too busy with what you're already doing? That's what this chapter is all about; because it's time we get accountable. Because the growth of your business is just as important as all the jobs on your never-ending to-do list.

What we really need is a timeline of how this vision becomes your reality. When I finally acknowledged and looked at where I was and how I was keeping myself there, everything changed. I needed to take back control of my whole life, but at my lowest, my aim was to get a handle on my day-to-day finances first because I knew that was the key for everything that needed to happen for me to change my life. To get out of those situations draining everything that I was. The strong woman I had within me, quietening her voice to suit someone else.

But to be able to change that situation, I needed to make a plan of how I would free up enough of my cashflow to create available money to pay for what we needed, as well as a plan to get rid of my debt. At this time, a huge portion of my income from my job was going towards minimum payments on credit cards. For me, it involved getting my ideas for running my own business off the ground so that I could make more money with the freedom of working for myself.

So, I started looking at what it would take to run my own business. Having worked with clients over the 12 years since I started doing this, it's evolved into a more structured system now, the MATHS® System that you're reading about in these pages, instead of just being my survival guide. Because getting on top of your finances isn't just about surviving.

But we need to get on with the next MATHS® lesson. To be clear, this chapter isn't about having an accountability buddy or checking in regularly with a peer, although that does have its place and can be really useful. This is about working towards keeping yourself accountable by applying the brakes on your business temporarily, and on a regular basis, so that you can see just exactly what is happening on the operational side of things. You can't be in control of what's happening under the bonnet, and making informed decisions of what needs to happen next, if you aren't really looking at how the business runs. It's about adopting that CEO mindset we touched on in the previous chapter.

It's this mindset that feeds directly into how you utilise your time for maximum benefit, not just minimum gain, and this will, of course, be reflected in the finances of the business. The groundwork you are going to do in this chapter flows into the action you take in the following three chapters, so take the time to work through this in as much detail as you can. I promise you will thank me later!

Holding yourself accountable, and continuing to work towards that North Star of yours, starts with knowing where you are now. Because change and improvement start with you, no one else will do this for you. Please don't feel overwhelmed by this. This isn't designed to make you feel that way and it's totally okay to go at your own pace. The key realisation is when you accept that only you can do this. This is your catalyst to say to yourself "well, if not now, then when?"

If you work for yourself in your own business, you'll know how lonely it can be while you're wearing all the hats and are responsible for making all the decisions:

- Pricing
- Branding
- Marketing
- IT
- Legal and compliance
- Regulatory requirements
- Bookkeeping
- Business development
- Credit control
- Relationship building
- Customer service

I'll stop now because I'm starting to get a nervous sweat on myself! But you get my point, the list is endless. It's very easy to feel overwhelmed by everything that you're not doing, because you're just one person and sometimes you feel like you're fighting against the world.

And let's not forget the non-business side of the demands on your time too. Like running a house, being present as a family member, being a good friend and, heaven forbid, there might be some time in there just for you. Sometimes.

So, let's break all of this down a little and see if we can't put this into perspective.

To be the CEO of your business, you need to be steering the direction of your business. This is so much more than being the busiest of busy bees, because without a helicopter view and overview of what's bringing the cash in, it will be easy to miss opportunities, drop balls and spend time focusing on less valuable, time-consuming tasks.

Now remember, money is an infinite resource.

Let me say that again, money is an infinite resource. There are lots of ways to make more money. Time, however, is finite and there are only so many hours in the day, so it's how you spend your time that is most important here as this is the rational limited resource.

It's the difference between what you're doing now versus what you want to be doing in the longer term. What you want now compared to what you want the most. The overarching vision.

So, the steps we need to work through here are as follows:

- What needs to be done in your business to grow it or even to run it?
- How long do each of these tasks take to complete?

- How long do we want to be working in our business, ideally?
- How much money do we want to be earning and why?
- What do we want to be actively doing in our business and what do we dislike doing?

Once we have these parameters established, we can start to build up a plan of how we can make all the pieces fit together and then make shifts in our business to make them happen.

What actually needs to be done for your business?

Be honest and realistic with yourself here.

You're going to need to carve some time out from being "in the business" to be able to do this effectively. Set yourself actual dates in your diary for business days and keep that time sacred for some 'working on, not in' time. And start by taking a long hard look at the tasks that are needed in order for your business to actually run. It will be very easy to put this off, but skipping steps here will only mean having to start from the beginning again later so I would recommend that you do this thoroughly to start with.

The Accountability part of the MATHS® system is about taking responsibility for everything that needs to be done, at the same time as acknowledging that you're worth investing in by getting the help and support for everything that you need done but can't do/don't want to do yourself. Because, as much as you pretend to be, you're not an octopus with eight arms that can function doing different eight different tasks at the same time.

So, get yourself a spreadsheet (my particular favourite medium for this sort of task!) or a notebook or a big piece of paper, and mind map all the aspects of your business that need to be taken care of.

A general list is fine. Looking at what others do in your industry and your network is also a good starting point if you can, but what is it that you do currently? Day-to-day, week-by-week, etc.

My preferred way to do this is to think about the experience that my customer has when working with me, from the first point of contact or enquiry, right through to the completion of a piece of work. For me, that can be a recurring service, such as monthly management accounts or annual corporation tax returns, or it can be a one-off piece of financial coaching or mentoring work for a set period. You want to run through all those services and offerings. Plus, how you actually get them through the door in the first place.

- How do those people find you? How do you capture their details?
- What might be the usual way that they will contact you? And how do you respond? Could there be some sort of automation or templates that could be used here?
- How do you currently on-board someone? Do they need to sign a contract? How do you record their personal information?
- How do you arrange times to meet with or speak to your clients?
- How do you contact them with queries and what system do you have in place to make sure they reply to you?

Do you get the picture? Hopefully, you'll also start to appreciate why it's important that you carve out some specific time for this exercise because it will require focus and is not the sort of thing that you can dip in and out of around other admin tasks, or dictate some notes into your phone while you're dealing with life admin.

You can totally expect to have additional things spring to mind at random times of the day too. Once you start to actually look at your internal processes analytically, you'll be having regular epiphanies throughout your day and even in the night, with brain drops of things you've forgotten and then remember out of the blue. At least, I did! Who knows, you might find this whole process a lot smoother!

Make life easy for yourself and set up a way that you can capture these lightbulb moments as they occur; somewhere that you can record them and save them for later, when it's actually convenient! And also in a way that will be easy for you to find them when you are back to working on your overview document. I now use Trello for this sort of thing, but I've been known to use my calendar to take notes and then I know where they all are when I need them. I also love a Bullet Journal, but I don't always carry this around with me, whereas my phone is generally not very far from my hand or back pocket!

As you work through your every day, you can compare this document to what you're actually doing. Are you recording the full picture of what's actually involved? Are you being realistic about all the tasks that are needed to do a thorough piece of work? Also, start to think about whether all the tasks you've recorded are actually necessary, or whether they're just something that you've always done without really questioning the value of them.

How long do each of these tasks take to complete?

As you are clearer now and have good visibility of what tasks are needed in your business, you can start to be more aware of the length of time things take to complete. Start to keep a track of these as accurately as you can when you carry them out.

Do you keep track of how long your work takes to complete as you go along? Do you keep timesheets? OK, this might just be the old traditional accountant in me coming out – we used to have to keep track of our time in 6-minute increments on timesheets that needed to be submitted each week!

This isn't just about the time you spend working with or on things for your clients, doing what you do best, working in your zone of genius. I want to know specifically, how much of your working week, or even your weekends and evenings, do you spend doing admin and other 'non-client facing' work that is still essential to the running of your business. Because so often we discount these things but they still take up valuable time.

The more detailed you can be with this, the more data you'll have to see exactly how long things take. This is an invaluable planning tool; because when you have a realistic view of this, you will be able to accurately plan your days and weeks without under-estimating how long a piece of work will take and then feeling like you're wading through treacle when you get to the end of the day having not completed as much as you'd hoped. No-one enjoys that feeling.

You can track time manually, and that's great if this works for you, but it can just feel like it's just adding another task to the to-do list (well, it does for me!), so if you are anything like me, I recommend using an app like Toggl or ClickUp to keep track.

ClickUp is a great app that allows you to plan ahead for your week (we'll talk more about this in the next chapter) by scheduling in your tasks, with estimated times for completion. It then has a timer function to record actually how long something took you, so this is great from a metrics and reporting point of view.

Ask yourself some honest questions, again, as you work through this list. Are these tasks that you're carrying out necessary within your business? Why are they an important part of the process when you work with clients? What problems do they solve that make the customer experience a better one? Or do you do them because you've always done them and are fearful of changing something that has become so comfortable?

This is something I see a lot, particularly with people that have been working in their industry for a good few years. They use the same processes that they learned when they were first starting out or as a trainee, because it's all they know and it's something they're comfortable with. We know all about this now, and how our brain works from the Mindset chapter, so the idea is to get curious and really question every part of what you do and why.

Our goal here is to get to the end of this task and to have a fully documented set of checklists or process maps for your entire business, whichever way you've worked through it. Soon, you will be able to clearly see all the parts that need to be carried out to get everything completed and do an efficient job, which in itself will save you time in the long run as you'll have full visibility of what needs to be ticked off for each piece of work you do. One of the super valuable reasons for having detailed process maps is to give you more confidence at some point in delegation and outsourcing. With a ready-made blueprint of the inner workings of your business, someone you trusted to get involved would be in for a super easy ride. You could even add in all the additional touches that you want in there to make your clients feel special and appreciated. Customer service often gets neglected when we get busy!

So, while you're analysing your time, you could take this one step further and get curious about how you're spending all your time. In for a penny, in for a pound, right? How often are you scrolling through your social media accounts? Or answering that email at 9pm before you start your favourite program. So, we are not just talking about the time you're sitting in your office in 'work-mode.' Could you be more efficient with the time outside of the office too? #justsaying

I don't bring this up to give you something to hit yourself over the head with and tell yourself that all you are doing is rubbish, by the way. We all lose time scrolling on social media, or reading news apps, or getting chatty on a call with a friend or client. But we are so often oblivious to all this, and how much of our precious resource that this absorbs. We need to create some awareness around it. Because with awareness comes the choice to make a change if you realise it isn't serving you, your clients, or your business.

How long do we want to be working in our business?

Depending on how accurately you've completed the first two parts of this exercise, you'll now be able to realistically see what needs to be done in your business, and how long it takes you to do it.

You'll be able to establish how many hours a week you'll need to work to service your current clients on a regular basis.

You'll be able to see at a glance what your spare capacity is for taking on new clients, and when you'll need to start a wait list for your services.

That is incredibly empowering stuff! The planning abilities you'll now have will mean you can be super clear with clients on their expectations of working with you, as well as managing suppliers, pricing considerations and future strategies for your cash flow forecasting.

We all know that the intention of starting our own business, as well as being able to provide financial security and independence, is to have some flexibility to be able to take time off when we want to for things like holidays, time with family, or to follow other interests. So now you know how long it actually takes to run your business, you may just surprise yourself at just how much time you spend in it because you just see it as "normal." You may well be able to take time to meet friends for lunch or take an afternoon off, but how often do you have to compensate for that by getting up with the lark to get those hours in beforehand, or by working a few extra hours late at night once the kids are in bed?

Let's park the work you've done so far in this chapter and look separately at just how long you want to be working in your business. Forget what you actually work, or what needs doing. How many hours feels like the amount of time that the CEO version of you is going to work?

Get yourself a year to view planner in a diary or print one off from your calendar app on your computer. Start marking out when you know or plan that you WON'T be available to work. School holidays, including inset days, will be available on your local council websites. Do you have any holidays already planned? Get all those dates scored out.

Once the 'known' dates are mapped out, you can start to think broader. Do you have a burning desire to take more time away from your business for enjoying life? Where's that flexibility we were just talking about? Maybe you want to start with a long weekend off a month, or every Friday off. Take a different colour pen or highlighter and mark that out. How would your workload fit into that new timeframe?

Remember, for now, this is an 'ideal situation' look at the planner. This is CEO mindset, so just stick with the process.

Because we've already looked at how long tasks take to complete, as well as how long you spend running your business, you can compare these with the hours you have available on your 'ideal work calendar.' If you took a look at your workload and clients now, how do the timescales compare or fit together? Could you manage your clients well with the time resource you want to work? Do you have scope for more clients? This will help you to realistically determine how many more, without overloading yourself.

It will also highlight quite quickly how realistic your current workload is compared to the dream CEO life you want to be living. If you are regularly catching up with tasks in the evenings and weekends, the chances are that your ideal schedule doesn't in any way match the reality of your situation.

More importantly, where does this leave time for all that working on the business instead of in the business? We know this is important, this is where the clarity appears.

So now what?

You could make the decision now that there aren't enough hours in the day for you to get through what's needed, and you could think about getting someone on board to support you in some capacity.

Or you could be worried about the cost of hiring someone to help. So, let's tackle this elephant from a different angle.

How much money do you want to be earning?

If the promise of highlighting where time can be saved in your business isn't a big enough carrot for you (I know things, remember? You've got those mindset gremlins getting a foothold into your thoughts, taking over, and pushing you in a certain direction without you even realising it), let's talk about the money side instead.

Let's recap: you now know what needs to be done in your business, and you know how long it takes. You have big dreams of how you'd rather be spending some of your time recharging as well as allowing space for ideas to flourish, so we know ideally how long we want to be spending on the work.

How does that measure up on the finances side?

So, you know the total hours you worked, on average, over each week/month/year, and you can compare that to the income you've earned/paid yourself over the same period. This will give you an average earning rate:

Take your income for the month (or week, depending on what timeframe you're looking at), without VAT, and divide it by the hours worked in that same timeframe; welcome to your average hourly rate!

An hourly rate is a good metric to determine whether your charging structure is reflective of the value you provide your clients, as well as a way of measuring what your time is worth to you. It can be quite the eye-opener!

When I work with clients on this for the first time, they are often quite shocked at what this number works out to be. Usually, this surprise comes down to one of two things:

- They don't have a handle on what goes into the whole client experience to know how to price their work for clients.
- They don't factor in all the hours that they spend in the business themselves. This can lead to overbooking, but will also massively drive your hourly rate down!

Now, if you're happy with this hourly rate, and the hours you work in your business, then congratulations, you can move on to the next chapter! Otherwise, stay tuned, my friend.

To help you interpret what this number/rate is telling you, the more hours you push into your working time for the same rate of pay, the less you are earning. If you pay yourself £1,000 per week, your hourly rate will be higher if you work 20 hours, than if you work 40 hours.

This rate is diluted by all the work and tasks that you do. All of them. Including the admin; the stuff you finish off but don't really call work because you have a glass of wine at your desk, or the TV on in the background.

Whilst you may have been telling yourself that you can do all the administrative side of your business because it's 'easy,' and you like to keep everything under control, that doesn't mean it's the best use of your time! It's normal to work like this when you first start out with your business, but living the boot-strapping life is not where you are now as the CEO. It's time to start thinking about the bigger picture.

But an hourly rate doesn't pay the mortgage, so let's look at this another way to give you another useful metric.

Let's start with the end result, because that's the best bit! How much money do you want to pay yourself each month? We can build up to figuring out what our North Star income figure looks like later, for now, let's think about a figure that would feel aspirational now. This is the first time we're dipping into talking about your numbers in any real detail.

Now, listen, there's no easy way to say this; you are going to have to get comfortable thinking about and exploring your numbers. If you don't feel ready at this stage, or the thought of it brings you out in a cold sweat, perhaps go back over the Mindset chapter and explore why. Use the journal prompts in the chapter to see if you can pinpoint where the worry comes from.

If you're not happy stabbing in the dark, let's start with what you currently pay yourself from the business. Take a quick look at your bank account to figure this out, or else take a look at the business bookkeeping records. What did you pay yourself into your own account from the business over the last year?

It's worth mentioning here that you will need to take your tax liability into account if part of how you pay yourself includes dividends. If you do this, you'll know that the tax owed on dividends is paid separately to HMRC when you file your tax return, so you need to factor this into your number.

Essentially, it's the number you have available to pay your bills, the mortgage, and the car payments. How much have you paid yourself after tax?

If you operate as a sole trader, you'll have something similar to consider in that your drawings from your business will also still have a tax bill needing to be paid.

With a starting point of your income for the last year, this will be a good enough place to begin with.

Ask yourself:

- Was the yearly figure enough to cover what you needed?
- Did your earnings cover all your bills and spending, without additional pressure or the need to draw more from the business?

You'll know if you needed to keep topping up your personal balances that what you pay yourself isn't enough for all your bills and spending, so notice your regular behaviour with your income, and just remember that nothing is 'bad,' at all.

When we have an awareness of habits and spending, we can make more use of planning and ensuring that tax efficiencies are considered. We'll look at this in more detail in the Housekeeping/Solutions chapters, but for now, we need a gauge on what feels like an aspirational income figure.

So, with this in mind, now make a decision on what an aspirational income target is. Is it a percentage increase, or a lump sum increase? How much extra would you really like to see in your own bank account? What could that mean to you if you think about spending power, or saving power?

With an annual target for income, it is then easy to break that down into a monthly and a weekly target.

OK, now you know how many hours you want to work - how does that fit in with the hours you've been working already?

If you are working too many hours compared to your ideal plan, how can you cut them back without impacting your income?

If you aren't bringing home enough money, how could you free up more time to do more income generating tasks? Or charge more for the work you are doing?

In most cases, you're likely to either need to consider increasing your pricing, and/or start to get serious about delegating, at least to some extent, to administrative support as a starting point. Remember, the goal is the CEO mindset!

If you find at this stage that the numbers and hours don't add up, you have all the information at your fingertips to start experimenting and moving the dial in different directions to find a balance that works for you. There are any number of 'what if' scenarios that you could play with here.

All in all, your North Star will guide you at each step. Once you have that clearly in view, you can ask yourself if your decisions take you closer to it, or further away. As an example, maybe you don't mind working all the hours in the short term if your goal is to build your business ready to groom it for sale. Maybe working less hours is more important to you because you want to spend more time with your children while they're small, so you're happy focusing on the smaller scale for now. But still, with this data at your fingertips, you'll know exactly which dial to crank up when it comes to upscaling your operations.

What tasks do we want to be doing in our business?

If you've reached the conclusion that you are going to go down the route of delegating or outsourcing some of your work, congratulations! It's a big step. You can now work through your process map and customer journey schedules that you prepared earlier. You will clearly be able to see what needs to be done, as well as being able to identify where processes can be streamlined!

Use highlighters, either on your paper notes or in a spreadsheet, to colour code the different parts of the work and services that you offer. Split them between the following four categories:

Colour 1 - Zone of genius

Colour 2 - What you like to do

Colour 3 - What you could do if you had to

Colour 4 - What you hate to do.

Keep a track of these, or better still, head to the book resources section of my website (link in the last chapter) and download the tasks matrix that I've got in there to scribble them down as you work through.

This will really highlight for you the tasks and work that you carry out that you are known for as the expert, the one to go to, the work you do that provides the transformation to your clients. You will also then see the peripheral tasks that need to be carried out and your appetite for doing them yourself.

Keep a tight hold of this list because as we start to pull your bigger picture plan together and think about how we're going to get you there in the quickest time possible, it's going to be important to recognise that you can't keep yourself sane, free from burnout and doing all the things for all the people, all by yourself. Smart people, who run their business as a CEO, delegate and build a team of people who can help them. They build a network, which helps to keep them accountable in their longer-term goals. They work smarter, not harder.

So, are there any tasks that you could delegate sooner rather than later? Maybe now's the time, when you are looking at the money in the bank, to use it wisely. Additional team members increase capacity so will help to boost the cash coming in. A simple comparison of the number of hours you could delegate at your own hourly rate against the cost of support will show you whether it's worthwhile investigating. Explore the possibilities, you never know where it could take you!

Pulling it all together

How does it feel now to have this aerial view of your business, as though it's not actually your business at all? As though you're viewing the goings on from a helicopter above the action. This is an absolutely perfect way to give yourself clarity, because by doing these tasks you remove the emotion from the everyday frustrations and see exactly how you'll be able to make clear, informed decisions to move your business in the direction you want. Depending on how you want it.

These exercises are just the starting point; once you've worked through all the different parts, choose a starting point and stick with it for a set amount of time. Say, three months, to start with. Because consistency will be really important for you in order to be clear on what has worked and what needs to be streamlined later.

Set dates in your diary now to review this; half a day or a full day to understand how your changes have improved things:

- How has your time management changed?
- What has been the impact on your income?
- Are you happy with the rates you charge for the work you do, and the time it takes you to do it?
- How has streamlining your customer experience affected your workflow?

When you're ready to make some tweaks, make one or two changes (making too many in one go means you'll find it hard to see what has worked or caused something to go wrong), and then leave for another period.

I'd love to know how you get on with this, you can email me on tanya@financialwingwoman.com.

6

TIMETABLING

This chapter is exciting, because we will be covering how to actually start taking action on what we need to get done and how we're going to build everything into your standard year. We've done some work on this already in the Accountability chapter. This will come in useful here as we can use all the information from there and create a timetable for how you are going to start working in your business as it continues to grow. Plus, we'll be breaking down what is actually needed to run your business so that you have a plan that you can keep referring back to as you start navigating this growth journey on your terms.

When I first realised the power that coming this far gave me, just with the mindset work and being able to quantify the time I spent in my business, it changed the game for me. It gave me the confidence to pull more of a structure together for my business; and not just my business - this became the blueprint for my whole life at the time. Birthdays, important events, payment deadlines and client commitments were all part and parcel of this system.

With so much uncertainty around the separation, my finances, and running my own businesses, these plans took everything out of my head, which gave me space to think and properly reset. Previously, thoughts would pop into my head at all hours of the day and night. I started to feel restful for the first time in a long time. And like I was finally back in control of the money coming in and out of my life. Whilst I didn't have everything all together by that point, because I still needed to implement it, I had the confidence of a plan that would get me there, so I was able to stop worrying so much.

With a flight plan and a checklist, you can just get it done, right? So, what's the big thing that holds you back the most?

For me, and for most of the people I speak to, it was about time. I don't have time.

How many times have you told yourself that?

"I don't have time to bring someone on board, it doubles the workload while they're being trained and I'm checking their work. I might as well just keep doing it myself."

"I don't have time to look at my finances, I've got fourteen other more important things to do before I consider poking needles in my eyes and looking at my bank statements. I'll do that in that on my next free weekend (that will never come)."

"By the time I finish work, I need to be present for the kids; sorting dinner, supervising homework, getting some housework done so the house doesn't feel like a bomb's hit it."

I hear you; the list is endless.

Whilst money is also a common reason people think they can't do something, at least money is something that we can take action to get more of. None of us, however, has the magic solution for limitless time. But time can be used more efficiently. You can implement things into your business to save you time, whether that's streamlining client systems, getting help or thinking about launching courses and programs as an alternative to solely working with clients on a 1-1 basis.

Time is the only finite resource we have in our business. Hours in the day, days in the week, time with your family and loved ones, time at work, time to build your own dreams. Whether you start now, or start next week, you have to start, so instead of telling yourself 'I don't have any time for this,' or 'it's on my to do list for when I get some more time,' let's just assume that you can if you really wanted to and focus on how having a financial flight plan might feel for you instead. Freeing? Powerful? Stable? Clear? Let's make some progress against that!

So, this chapter is about being honest with how you're spending your time, getting detached from your role in this and mapping out how you're going to use the time you have to maximum effect. We've already mapped out what it takes to run the show in the Accountability chapter. This is about giving you tools to have control over your time.

We also need to build an actual timetable of what is non-negotiable in your business and is going to happen regardless so that you have complete visibility of what's coming up. This way, you won't get blind-sided by what's around the corner. Everyone needs a plan.

One of the biggest things that I learned from timetabling was the conscious act of questioning at each opportunity – do I really need to be doing this? Does this get me closer to my North Star? Ask yourself the same thing. Are you doing something because you've always done it? Is it a good use of your time? Does it serve you? Could you do it differently?

And this is where the concepts of the MATHS® System overlap and you'll juggle multiple elements of it through the journey. Because I am going to ask you now to question yourself:

Mindset – is this a safety blanket? It's what you know, and would you be able to save time by either not doing that unnecessary task, or by delegating it?

Accountability – ask for help. Hold yourself accountable, and ask your network – is there a better way? What would the solution be?

And now the Timetabling - let's remind ourselves of why this is important. How can you manage your money if you don't know when cash payments and receipts are due?

How can you work out how much money you can make if you don't know how many hours you are going to work? Or how many hours you have the physical capacity to work because life is in the way?

And what if you make awesome plans, with phenomenal growth expected, to then realise that you just need to find an extra 45 hours a week to achieve it?

Being your own Wingwoman means having your eyes wide open at all times. We don't bury our head in the sand, and we face up to what's in front of us. However scary that might feel, it is never as bad as you think it's going to be.

Because when you know what steps are coming, or what's around the corner, you can take action.

How do you think it would feel to know in advance exactly what you need to do for your business and when? If you always have the end date/deadline in mind, you can work backwards and make sure you have also allowed adequate time so that you're properly prepared.

When it comes to Timetabling for your business, there is a lot that we do actually know in advance, so with awareness and time, there's no reason you can't be ahead of the game and using timetabling skills will give you back control.

Let's look at these from a few different perspectives.

An annual timetable

We touched on this in the earlier chapter when we talked about using an annual planner to mark out the times when you know you won't be available to work.

I want you to go back to this now and take a look at what you've blocked out. Hopefully, this plan will give you a boost and help you to think about how you can balance your work with your personal plans. So much of the work we need to do in this book crosses over both business and personal, so it makes sense to not just consider the business side of things. Because at the end of the day, we may be the CEO, but this is still our baby and we are the ones showing up for it.

But we also want to make sure the personal side is as stress-free as possible, without thoughts

constantly popping into your head questioning whether you're on top of everything, doing it right, so we need to get a handle on the business side.

To start with, we need to know what deadlines we have that are immovable? Once you can see when something needs your attention, then you can work backwards and mark out time for preparation and planning to achieve whatever you are working on because time needs to be scheduled for that too. How long do you really need for that? Remember your time tracker? Have you realistically allocated the time you need or underestimated it, which will cause you friction in the future?

Accounts and tax returns:

Company/business year end

You will be able to find out when your company accounts and corporation tax return need to be done and submitted, based on the filing deadline of the official documents. You'll also know from the beginning when your tax bill needs to be paid.

If you don't know this, it's always nine months after your company year-end date.

So, with a December year-end date, you'll need to be ready with the accounts and a payment for the tax man by the end of September.

There is a possible exception to this in your first year, so check with Companies House for when this is. Once you have the dates, go ahead and mark that in the planner.

You can check Companies House here:

https://www.gov.uk/government/organisations/companies-house

Just stick your company name in here and it will tell you what you need to know about the important dates and your deadlines.

If you employ an accountant to complete the company accounts for you, and I'm assuming that many, if not all of you will, then you can have a chat with them about when they plan to do their work for you to keep you on the straight and narrow.

You will need to balance making sure that you have everything for the year to complete the accounts and records, without leaving everything to the last minute to allow time for them to complete their work. I would recommend ensuring this is completed around three months after your year end, so take a look at your calendar and allocate time to complete this specific task.

Personal tax returns for directors and sole traders

Personal tax responsibilities are just as important as the company dates. Just to confuse us all, these filing deadlines are different to company ones.

The tax year for individuals always runs from 6th April to the following 5th April, so the date of 5th April should be noted on your calendar as the end of the tax year. This is important to highlight so that you can take advantage of tax planning before-hand, such as paying into ISAs or pensions, as well as any extra dividends, depending on your personal tax position. Your accountant will be able to guide you more with this, and we'll also cover it in the Housekeeping chapter.

The filing deadline for getting your self-assessment tax return in, as well as paying any tax due is 31st January following the end of the tax year. Make sure this payment deadline is on your calendar.

If your tax bill is more than £1,000, and the tax due isn't taken before you are paid, like it is with a salary, then you will likely also need to pay payments on account for tax. These are due twice a year; on 31st January and 31st July. Another date for you - mark these dates in.

Employer payroll annual returns

If you run a payroll through your business, whether just for yourself or for employees, you'll have annual filing and payment responsibilities for this. This is in line with the tax year end, so anchor these responsibilities in with the income tax deadline and kill two birds with one stone! You'll need to make sure you complete all payroll year-end procedures for your employees by 31st May, and file any returns related to benefits in kind by 6th July. Mark all these dates; forewarned is forearmed!

Other important annual dates; these dates will be personalised to you.

When I first started my business, I felt like I was cheating to some extent. I knew all about things like making sure I had insurance, and who I needed to register with because I'd already watched lots of businesses go through the same process as part of my role as an accountant in practice. If you aren't aware though, some things are easy to miss, so here are some other things to keep on your radar.

Registration and renewal with the Information Commissioner Office (ICO). If you process personal information you will need to register with the ICO according to part of the Data Protection Act, regardless of the size of your business.

Having a limited company means that you'll need to file a compliance statement with Companies House annually. This just makes sure that details like the registered office address and personal details of directors are up to date and still accurate. Check on the Companies House website for when this is due on your individual company record. You can register for email alerts for your company on the website, so make sure you take full advantage of this!

What about important renewal dates, such as insurance, memberships, licenses, subscriptions? How often do these payments surprise you because you forget when they're coming out of your bank on auto-renewal? Even if you do have a relatively good handle on your cash flow, this won't mean much if all relevant items aren't factored in on your timetable. Mark time to review these at least a month before the renewal date. If work is required to go with renewals, such as submission of CPD reports for professional memberships, or checking the clauses and adequate cover for insurance, then again, build this time into your calendar ahead of the renewal date so that you can be prepared.

Mark each of these dates in the calendar so that you have full visibility of them. Whilst it may help with cash flow to pay for these monthly, you can often secure discounts for annual payments on some expenses, so it's worth exploring which is better value for you.

How many things creep up on you and you aren't prepared for them that perhaps extend beyond a year? Add some notes in your planner with important dates that can be carried forward to next year and beyond so that you don't lose sight of them. Examples include:

- Break clauses in contracts and agreements
- PCP finance arrangements on cars
- Leasing of property or premises
- End dates of payment plans
- Finance agreements
- Loan payments

At the risk of repeating myself, because this is so important, make sure you plan in time for review! Not just ahead of when renewal anniversaries come around, but to check in on your overall business performance. How did last year go? How many problems or forgotten things crept up to bite you? What can you improve for the following year? What plans do you have for the business? Make this part of your plan and mark out the time in your planner.

Most importantly, check in on your progress towards your North Star. Are you moving in the right direction? Are you where you expected to be? What changes could you make now to improve your position by this time next year? Is it time to update your vision board? When it comes to putting a bigger game plan together, such as your strategy for the year, we'll cover that in the Solutions chapter.

Quarterly timetable

- VAT returns

If you're VAT registered, I'm sorry to tell you this, but this is another one of those obligations where you just don't have any excuse for not knowing when these are due to be completed and filed. It's easy to look up, and you need to know, so let's get ahead of it before it becomes a problem. Once registered, your VAT certificate will tell you exactly when the quarter dates are that you need to take notice of, and you will have one month and 7 days to get your return filed and the liability paid across to HMRC.

If you can't find your VAT certificate, you can download it from your Government Gateway account. Don't have this set up? It's time you did; don't rely on your accountant to be able to access this for you. This is vital company data that you should know how to put your hands on. And don't forget to get your calendar updated! When you know it needs to be completed, make sure you schedule in the time to get it done, or delegate it to someone else.

- Management accounts

If you don't do these monthly, then schedule in some time to go through your numbers on a quarterly basis, even if it's just the key figures to highlight where you can spend your time efficiently.

The key numbers are highlighted for you in the Housekeeping section.

- Dividend planning

You can also take some time to schedule in reviewing your own remuneration, to include payments on dividends and benefits in kind, but we'll cover that in more detail in the Housekeeping chapter.

- Quarterly planning

Quarterly planning makes perfect sense; if you break the year up into four chunks, you have 4 x 13-week periods. Split that into 12 weeks of action, and 1 week to review, and you've got a much more manageable timeframe to work and plan with! A 12-week action plan is more achievable, and this format allows you to update your plans as you work through the overall year. Because you will be able to react to opportunities, there is never a better time to be building in working on your business as well as in it. By scheduling and protecting your time for doing this ahead of the game, you'll have no excuses. Remember, no one is going to do this for you.

Break your quarterly goals down into monthly and weekly tasks to build up to getting this done so that the overall task doesn't feel quite so overwhelming.

For example, let's say one of your goals for Q2 is to get your tax return completed. You allocate one hour a week to get this done, and you can use the work that you did for your last tax return as a template.

ASK YOURSELF:

- What information did you need?
- Where did you find it?
- If you couldn't find it, and you had to search, set up a 'tax return info' document to list all the important information to make it easier for yourself next year. Better yet, while you're working on this year's tax return, for the tax year just finished, start setting things up for next year while it's fresh in your mind (notice what you need RETROSPECTIVELY to plan PROACTIVELY).
- As important documents come to you in the post/on email, save or scan them in an easy to find folder on your desktop, or wherever you will be able to find it without having to search endlessly for it when you need it.
- Once you have a plan for completion (this can be your first week's task in the quarter), allocate the different elements to each week.
- For example, one week could be to review and analyse your bank statements, another week could be to find and download your interest statements, finding details of child benefit or SEISS grants received.
- Before you know it, you're at the end of another quarter, and you've ticked a big frog off your list. Big pat on the back for you!

HERE IS a suggestion as to the sorts of things you could include in your business for managing your time, with themes for each.

Q1

Jan - Mar

- Review of Q4 - what are you bringing forward into Q1 of the new year?
- What is your timetable for the year looking like?
- Set up your shop front - what are your offerings? Facebook page? Website?
- What are your pricing strategies? Do they need to increase now, or in Q2?
- Setting your budget/forecast for the year
- Pension/ISA top ups before the tax year end

Q2

Apr - Jun

- Review of Q1 - what worked, what would you change?
- Plan for completion of tax return for tax year just ended
- Get your financial systems in place for the new financial year.
- Notice what you need retrospectively to plan PROACTIVELY
- Think about summer plans/managing through the school holidays

Q3

Jul - Sep

- Review of Q2 - what worked, what would you change?
- 6-month review of the numbers, 1/2 yearly check point
- Set up money pots - current year tax liability, forecasting for 2020/21
- Use the time through the holidays to plan your content strategy
- What offerings can you put out in September/new academic year to hit Q4 at a sprint?
- Mindset as we come into the final months of the year.

Q4

Oct - Dec

- Review of Q3 - what worked, what would you change?
- What do you need to do to pull everything over the line for this year?
- If you could start the year again, what would you do differently - leading into Q1.
- Use the Christmas season for connection, offerings and plans for next year.

Monthly timetable

- Quarterly planning actions

Don't forget to slot in your allocated time here from the quarterly planning schedule. If this only takes you an hour a week, imagine how much time it will save you, and the stress and anxiety that goes with it.

- Monthly management accounts

Monthly management accounts are great to keep on top of, along with making sure that you are invoicing your clients regularly. How often do you get to the middle of the month, or at least a week or so in, and find that you haven't even raised your invoices for last month? It's no wonder that you feel as though you never have as much in the bank to show for all the work that you put in!

If you don't send out your invoices for people, how will they know when they need to pay you?

- Credit control

And then there's always the credit control side. It's one thing to get those invoices out to clients for work completed, but what about checking that the client has actually paid you too? This all takes time, and it's important that you are on top of this.

Allowing clients space, or not communicating with them because you're uncomfortable chasing, or because they've said the 'cheque is in the post,' doesn't help anyone. Why should you cover the cashflow needs of your clients, and they themselves are only storing up problems for bills that will increase if they don't get a handle on their own cash management? Allowing your invoices to build up won't help and you're less likely to get paid the higher that balance becomes.

- Client reviews

If this is a regular issue for you, take some time to think about the type of clients you want to work with; clients that don't respect the time and effort you put into their work by being respectful of your payment terms are likely to be more difficult to work with. Do you want these in your life? If you take notice of the clients that habitually pay late, make unreasonable demands and aren't respectful of the time that goes into managing their work, you could consider the possibility that your life would be easier without these clients taking up your time, and actually make more space for the clients that you want to work with; those who pay you on time, respect your rates and the effort it takes to complete your work. How good does that sound?

- Payroll

If you run your business through a limited company, or employ members of staff, then you'll need a payroll scheme set up in order to be able to pay them and yourself, as a director. Getting this processed and filed under the HMRC Real Time Information (RTI) scheme is really important and will save you the inconvenience of a fine and penalty for late processing.

- Expenses claims

Make sure that you review your personal bank/credit card statements to incorporate any business expenses that you want to recoup from the company by way of an expense claim. Include in this mileage claims and your portion of the business cost for use of home as office, if applicable. By doing this on a monthly basis you'll be able to remember costs, journeys and any other relevant information that needs to be stored when it comes to claiming this as part of a legitimate business record. Monthly expense claims are ideal as a memory jogger; I keep the details of specific journeys and expenses as a note to the event in my calendar app on my phone. A quick review of my diary for the month then usually gives me most of what I need for any claims.

- General planning – what is on the horizon for you this month?

I always spend time at the beginning of each month mapping out what needs to be done and achieved. My regular recurring client work goes in here, my own admin, and when I know I have appointments and time away from the office and home. Filling the available time and reminding yourself that there are only so many hours in the day is so important – remember, you aren't super-human!

The more of an aerial view you get of your business (let's call it Operation Helicopter), the clearer your monthly plan will be. And the more organised you'll feel.

Sometimes it feels as though you're repeating the effort (wait, you want me to do this annually, quarterly, monthly…), but the regular checking and reviewing all serves to help you question whether something is actually necessary or working. Doing something monthly that could be done quarterly? Great, shift it out and pat yourself on the back for being more efficient and saving yourself that monthly time, whilst still getting the results you need.

Rinse and repeat

Roll this out to give you a weekly and daily plan too. Taking control of your business is about more than the finances.

Remember that time is the most limited of resources, so be as frugal with that as you can and your future self will thank you for it.

I use a Bullet Journal to plan out monthly, weekly and daily tasks, so do check the book resources section of my website for a link to this.

Other time saving hacks that have saved my sanity

Back in the days when I was managing my fledgling business, it felt as though I never had a moment to myself, I was working in financial training part time to support me financially and manage my debt, juggling spending as much time as possible with my daughter, whilst being out with my new found friends to keep my sanity in check. All the while, also formally severing the ties I had with my ex and all the legal shenanigans that brought to the table. It was a lot, and I would regularly sit at my desk in the corner of my room, late at night, and just stare at the blank screen of my laptop without knowing what to do first/next.

I would sometimes literally feel as though I was in a flat spin, like something out of Top Gun. Whatever I chose to do, all I could think of was all the tasks I wasn't doing and every ping on my phone made me anxious because who could that be chasing me, and what have I not done now?

What I eventually learned to do, and I regularly remind myself of doing this now, is making a habit of both time blocking and task batching.

Time blocking

With the structure we've already gone through, and knowing with certainty what needs to be done and when, you will clearly see what time you have available for everything to be done. You'll hopefully also have a list of all the tasks for running your business, and realise that there are tasks that can be delegated so you can have more of your own time back.

Time blocking involves dividing up the time you have available into blocks of time, with each block specifically earmarked for completing a specific task, or group of similar tasks. This might be a piece of project work for a client, meetings, or blocks of admin time to respond to emails and other such things.

Set yourself up for the week on a Sunday evening, or early on a Monday, with what you know you have coming up for the week ahead. This takes the thought required out of what to do next, as you'll have a schedule to work with, and you'll no longer be dealing with a random to-do list.

Make sure you build in a bit of slack for unknowns and overruns that are inevitable, time to clear emails, and factor in things like lunch and realistic travel times, where appropriate.

The most important thing is to make sure that, at the end of each time block, you move on to the next thing on your schedule, even if you haven't finished all the work. Alongside the work that we've carried out in the Accountability chapter, this will help you get super clear on just how long things take to complete in your business. This will mean that you're charging fairly for your time, being efficient, as well as consciously streamlining the tasks involved in getting things done. In addition, you'll be able to more accurately time block going forward.

At the end of each working day, review how your time blocking has gone and shuffle the rest of the week accordingly. It's OK to move things into the following week; this gives you the chance to be proactive and let others know if this will impact them. Being able to manage expectations is a key part of your clients coming to rely on your word.

Task batching

Task batching is about grouping together all similar tasks and work so that you can be efficient with your efforts and limit the amount of context switching you have to do throughout your day. If it's any kind of admin, answering emails or time on your own business, aim to block this together in one time block. Invoicing clients, or returning phone calls, again batch these. Writing blog posts, social media content or taking care of your financial reviews, batch these all together at the same time.

Day theming

Day theming is another extension of this. Instead of batching tasks, or allocating time to certain things that need to be done, theming your days is about leaving all similar tasks to the one day when you know you will be able to devote the attention needed to it. For me, I aim to keep Mondays and Fridays for my own company admin, so I block my work calendar for clients to be able to contact me on Tuesday – Thursday only. I try to take care of my social media content either on the weekends, or a Monday and try to clear emails and finalise work on Fridays, as well as planning the following week/month.

Why have I gone through so much detail of what time you have available so far? It's important to be able to see both what needs to be done and when, and how much time you realistically have available to get it done. Using a visual tool of an annual, quarterly, and monthly planner meant I could see at a glance, whenever my heart rate started to escalate, that I was actually in control.

I had a plan to get everything done, and when I did look and realise that I had double or even triple booked myself (it happens, we all do it) I could take positive action and do something about it, instead of letting people down, or pulling an all-nighter, which I've also been known to do more than I'd like to admit. I could have that conversation with someone and rearrange, I could pick up the phone and negotiate an extension on deadlines, or commitments.

I could have control, and not allow it to take over and cost me more in my own well-being. And by being fully aware of realistically how long things take to complete (as we've worked on in the Accountability chapter), I could set up a plan of what could be achieved in the time I had available, and I could always deliver on time, or even ahead of schedule.

Whilst, as the name The Financial Wingwoman would suggest, the emphasis of the work I do is on finances, I can't emphasise enough how much your work on the finances of your business is only a part of the bigger picture. Most people focus on what they do best; it's human nature. It makes us feel good, we like to get good results, and we get paid well for the work that we do. The peripheral stuff can be handled by others.

But the thing is, with money, if you can't manage £100, you'll never be able to manage £10,000. It's the reason why lottery winners rarely manage to hang on to their fortunes. Mindset, accountability, and managing our time are also essential foundations for running successful businesses, as well as standing us in good stead with our personal lives. This then makes working on your finances so much more effective. There's absolutely no reason whatsoever that these tools can't, and wouldn't, help you with your time at home, and your personal finances. Give it a go and see how you get on.

While we're talking about time for our personal lives, let's not forget about making time for you. Part of keeping yourself accountable is making you a priority. You can't be the CEO of your business if you are out of action from burn out or constant illness from not taking care of yourself. This isn't selfish, or a luxury; it's a necessity.

Whilst I was trying to figure out how I would juggle everything, I found small hacks to help me free up some time at home too, so here are some of my favourite tips for you to try.

I'd love to hear yours so email me at tanya@ financialwingwoman.com or you can find me on Instagram @thefinancialwingwoman - drop me a message and let me know!

Whilst these won't free up 40 hours a week, we just need to start building you some small pockets of time where you can keep that time sacred for what you need to get done, just for you.

- Meal prep and delivery services
- After school clubs, play date circles
- Domestic help, including cleaners and laundry services
- Negotiate with your other half to see what they could take off your load to help
- Consider your sleep pattern - I get up earlier than

everyone else. That time of absolute silence from 5am is golden for me. Even the cats don't bother - it's all mine! Use it for you, an hour or two on your business when you need it will give you the most amazing boost to your day and when everyone else is stirring you've already got 2 hours under your belt. That's 10 hours a week!

7

HOUSEKEEPING

OK, now we're getting to the finance part, the things that we've maybe been avoiding dealing with. I've brought you on a journey though, through all the other processes first, so thank you for trusting me with this so far. What you've actually done is understand where you are with the resources you have available.

Resources.

I'll say that again. You know where you are with the resources you have available to you.

We've covered mindset, the stories we tell ourselves, and how you can perhaps start to think like the CEO you are meant to be.

We've dealt with what needs to be done in your business, and covered the fact that the buck stops with you. You need to hold yourself accountable, take responsibility and ownership of your business, and surround yourself with people who can help you get to where you want to be.

Remember, you can't wear all the hats all of the time.

We've looked at what time you have available, and how you can manage it, as one of the truly finite resources that you have to juggle.

But there's a reason that the finance side is lower down in the list of things to work with. If we jump straight into the area that people try and avoid the most, I would have lost you several chapters ago. There's a reason M is Mindset and not Money Management! Our thoughts and feelings around money are often the very reason that we don't like to deal with it. It makes us uncomfortable for all kinds of reasons.

Understanding where you are with your finances is one of the biggest stumbling blocks that I see so often and help a lot of my clients with. A lot of it stems from money mindset issues, or limiting beliefs picked up along the business journey.

Talk of the tax man can strike fear in the heart of many. That official, government presence and true authority that stands as a shadow in your peripheral vision can hang over you like a cloud and make you doubt whether what you want to achieve is OK or even allowed.

Imagine, as a child, overhearing a conversation from a parent or distant family about how dealings with the tax man have affected their business. Think about how that might stay with you. How that might affect the decisions you take, or the way you approach your finances.

No matter what, all the while you ignore or even refuse to have an awareness of the tax side of running your business, your entrepreneurial mindset, skills, and talent will only get you so far. It is absolutely key to growing, being successful and building the life you want.

Hopefully, this isn't something that you struggle with now; if memories of conversations such as these have held you back, you've worked through our Mindset chapter and you can start to recognise that the stories we tell ourselves often aren't our own baggage, and we've already done so much work through these chapters so far.

I want you to see the money part as almost the easy bit now. And we'll work on making best friends with the tax man too, because when you know the rules, the sexy strategies are easy!

Let's make a start!

If someone told you the path to untold wealth and abundance was in your bank statements, would that make it easier to review them on a regular basis?

If you read that the path to complete harmony with HMRC was to open that brown envelope and pick up the phone, would it make you more likely to do it?

The thing is, fear and emotion are at the foundation of dealing with money and finances.

We remove fear with knowledge.

When you know, you know. And you can start to make a plan with the resources that you have. It's not what you earn that makes you rich, it's what you do with it that does that for you. Whatever the situation; pension or no pension, credit card debt or debt-free, regular saver or perpetual spender, it doesn't matter. You can't make a plan of action if you don't know your starting point, and we start with knowledge.

You've already done a lot of this work. You have a lot of knowledge now about the inner workings of your business and what it takes to run it. Information that you perhaps didn't really consider as that important before. You know how many hours are needed to run your business, and you know how many hours you have and are prepared to give. Where there are any gaps, you can take action; take on more work, or delegate the non-essential tasks that don't need your undivided attention.

The same can be said with money. When you know, you have power. You have control.

We remove emotion with systems.

Emotion is the part of our unconscious brain that takes over and tries to keep us safe by hijacking our thoughts. The irrational part of our brain that senses when we feel nervous of the brown envelope that's just landed on the door mat, and convinces you that you will escape imminent death if you hide that envelope in the drawer in the hallway. How many times have you done this, and then tackled that letter, only to find it wasn't as bad as you thought it would be?

I used to have a client that flat out refused to open any brown envelopes. He would forward them all on to me and pay me to deal with them instead. He wouldn't even read the return address on the back, so the paperwork I used to deal with sometimes bordered on comical. Car tax refunds from the DVLA, TV licence renewal notices, income tax refunds, as well as the standard tax code notices and statements on account from HMRC. By hiding away from the monster in the envelope, we give it more power over us, and it becomes this huge demon that we can't cope with.

What is it that Hermione Granger said? "Fear of a name only increases fear of the thing itself." So true!

Putting a system in place to deal with things allows us to remove the emotion from the situation and we can think rationally about how we respond to it. The same way we can avoid drowning in our to do list by using a system like time blocking. We don't need to get lost in the overwhelm, we can simply follow a system and take any thought required out of the equation.

Now, I'm aware that this chapter gets a bit heavy with the explanation. Some of this is reference only, so it's useful to know but if you don't have any desire to understand what makes up different parts of financial statements, and why they're useful, skip straight to the section headed up 'Key metrics to watch – the non-negotiables' instead.

Financial statements – so what?

I prepare accounts for my clients on the accountancy side of my business. It's something I've known how to do and I've been working on for almost 25 years now. It's like with most things, like learning to drive or ride a bike; when you know how to do something, you don't question how it's actually done. So preparing accounts comes easily to me. It's a process, sometimes it's a bit of a puzzle, but there is a logical way through preparing them.

It is only as I've really come to understand how money mindset can impact my clients that I've started to appreciate how seemingly official pieces of financial paperwork can be so daunting. For me, at the start of turning my financial situation around, it was dealing with the debt that had this impact on me. A credit card statement on the doormat used to make me feel sick (thank goodness they went paperless!). In this chapter I want to cover the questions that I get asked the most about dealing with the finances of running a business.

Financial statements include the three main summary documents for businesses that give an overall picture of business performance over time.

They include - the profit and loss account, the balance sheet, and the cash flow statement.

The Profit and Loss Account

The **profit and loss account (P&L)** shows a summary of the profit or loss over the period. This is usually a full year.

To work out the profit or loss, you start with the total of the income, and then list down all the costs and expenses accumulated for the same period.

This will detail sales generated from business activities, along with the costs and overheads associated with creating that income.

What is useful about the P&L?

If you look at one period in isolation, the P&L account will show you the **margin** you are making on your goods and services; what you sell.

Splitting the costs between what you spend on buying products you plan to sell, or on paying other people to deliver services on your behalf, will give you more insight still. These are called

direct costs; by keeping these types of costs separate from general business costs, like marketing and premises costs, we can see the difference between gross and net profit margins.

The **gross profit margin** tells us how much profit we're adding onto the materials and products we buy to sell on, and the profit we make on services we bring in for our clients.

If we buy a candle for £10, and we sell it for £15, then we've made a £5 profit.

Take the gross profit figure, divide it by the sales figure, and then multiply it by 100 to get a percentage. This is the gross profit margin.

So, with our candle example, we have a profit margin of 33%.

We need to make a gross profit to cover all the other costs and overheads. Like you didn't already know that! But this margin is a great metric to keep track of over time to show what percentage in profit is being made.

Have you noticed that the margin is falling? That could be because your material costs have increased, but you haven't put your prices up. By measuring the metric, you can manage the outcome. If we do it regularly enough, we can spot a potential problem before it does any damage to your profit.

How much of a margin do you allow on top of your direct costs in your business pricing model?

This is a great question. Do you consider all the costs of running your business when you price your services? Do you even have a full awareness of what the costs are?

To work this out, you need to actually know what your other business costs are. What do you spend on things like advertising and marketing, admin support, travel costs, bookkeeping fees and so on? When you price your services, do you think about all of these costs too?

Take a look at your last set of accounts and turn to the P&L page. Or go and look at your bookkeeping software and check the latest numbers.

To be making a profit overall, by creating a **net profit**, your income has to cover all the costs, with some left over. If it doesn't, you've made a loss.

The more of an awareness you have of your overall costs, the more accurate your pricing will be. And the more control you'll have over your profit and, ultimately, the cash in the bank. There will always be other factors that impact this as well just to highlight this, such as what your competitors in your industry are charging, and what your customers expect to pay.

If you're interested, you can use the formula for the gross profit to calculate the net profit, with a bit of a tweak.

Take the net profit figure, divide it by the sales figure, and multiply the answer by 100 to get a percentage. This is the net profit margin.

How much, as a percentage, do you have left after you've paid out for all the costs associated with running your business? As with the gross profit percentage, you can track this over time. It will highlight for you when costs are increasing, if you aren't already aware, so you can

The Outlier – Dividends

One of the major advantages of running your business through a limited company is that you can be flexible about how you pay yourself as a director.

You can split this between salary and dividends. Now, your salary and associated costs are included in the P&L, but dividends aren't.

There's nothing to stop you creating your own version of your business 'profit' as a management figure, and including the dividends paid within it. This will give you your true business costs, for your own reference.

If part of your journey to your North Star is to be able to extract as much cash as possible out of your business, this metric including dividends could be something that you decide you want to keep your eye on to monitor how it changes over time.

When you're reviewing your figures, like the CEO you are, you will soon realise that once you've figured out your margins, looking at one year's figures in isolation is limiting and won't tell you very much. P&L figures become more useful if they're tracked over a longer space of time. Year on year, quarter by quarter, month by month.

Do these margins improve over time? What influences how they change? Can you spot a pattern? Are they higher at certain times of the year? What action can you take? Does it indicate that your prices could be increased? Or are your costs out of kilter for what you make?

Once you have this raw data, you can start to make changes. You can start to see what works for you, and what doesn't work so well so that you can walk it back if need be.

When you have more data available, you can start to compare individual elements of the P&L account too. Ask yourself questions, such as:

- How much are you spending on marketing? How does this compare to percentage increases (hopefully!) in sales?
- Could you change your marketing strategy and see if that improves profit margins? What works? What doesn't work?
- Had a stellar year two years ago? What was different then? What has changed since, and can the former successful year be replicated?
- Did you have help from someone, or the guidance of a coach?
- How do your freelance/outsourced costs change over time? Does that positively impact your profit?

The key thing to note with all of this is that **what gets measured gets managed**. And the key to being able to make decisions based on these figures and results is, firstly, knowing what they actually are.

The other key result of a P&L account is that this is the basis of your corporation tax calculation, for both limited companies and income tax for sole traders.

Having an awareness of the tax as you go along is important, so as not to fall foul of missing out on planning for the inevitable bill that will come with a profit, so we'll look at this later in the Solutions chapter. It's also an important part of what should be considered in your pricing. **Not all of the money you earn is yours.**

The Balance Sheet

The **balance sheet** shows a summary of assets and liabilities at the exact date of the year end, like a snapshot photograph at that single point in time.

This is effectively the net worth of the company and shows all the assets (such as equipment, computers, cash in the bank, stock and money that is expected in from customers) and the money owed to others (such as what's owed to suppliers, bank overdrafts, loans, and the amount due in tax to the various tax offices).

What is useful about the balance sheet?

This is good for showing the liquidity of a company, so how cash-rich is it? Or how much debt is it holding when compared to the assets? Obviously, if the liabilities (amounts owed out) are higher than the assets (amounts held or owed in), then this isn't good news. If an unexpected bill came in, without sufficient cash levels, a company might struggle to cover the payment without further increasing its debt or needing to borrow from the bank .

As your own personal company, whilst there are ideals in the big wide world, what is important about the balance sheet numbers is what they mean to you, and how they factor into helping you achieve your goals.

Other than keeping an eye on overall cash balances and any payments of bills and liabilities as they fall due, a useful metric is to keep an eye on is the amount due in from your clients at any time, if this applies to you. This is called the trade debtors, or receivables, figure.

The higher this number is, the more risk there is of you not being paid. As cashflow is a hugely important metric, this feeds directly into that, and how smoothly your business can run.

Having an effective credit control process in place will help you keep this on track, such as:

- Make clear your payment terms to your clients
- Make sure your invoices are sent out promptly
- Implement staged invoicing for project milestones or in advance
- Employ someone to take over the credit control function for you

Cash Flow Statement

Finally, the **cash flow statement** reflects the physical movement of cash for the business over the course of the year. This doesn't actually form part of a usual statutory set of accounts for a small business but can easily be found in any accounting software reports section.

The cash flow statement doesn't reflect profit at all, instead it deals with physical cash in and out of the bank account. It breaks down for you the balance in the bank account at the beginning of the year/period you're reviewing, compared to at the end of the year/period, and what has happened in between.

Things you could expect to see in here are cash boosts, such as funds from shareholders/owners and borrowings, as well as money spent on buying new equipment, repayment of debt and the general spending that's needed in running the business on a day-to-day basis.

If clients pay later than expected, this can mean the difference between having enough cash in the bank to be able to make payroll payments at the end of the month, as well as pay the office rent on time, or not. Knowing the cash flow position as far in advance as possible, and trying to plan for the certainty of uncertainty, is the best insurance policy a small business can have.

The key metrics to watch – the non-negotiables

Getting used to looking at your key financial reports is an ideal way to keep on top of what's important to you within your business. You don't have to stick to the official reports I've mentioned so far; they can be as simple as you like. Any important numbers to you can be part of your own **internal management accounts**. These are just for you, and as part of your role of managing your company, these will help you with decision making.

Do you want to know an estimate of the tax you might need to pay based on this month's profit figure? You can include that in your regular numbers to watch.

How about how much income and profit you've made, broken down by client? Then include that too.

Do you feel better if you know how much you need to save to cover your personal tax bill from the dividends you've just drawn? This can go in there too. It can include absolutely anything you want to know.

If you use accounting software then you will be able to use the functions in there to automatically run any of the financial statements that we've talked about, but if you don't have these, or don't really understand what these mean even if you can access them, you can make a start by just keeping an eye on the following three non-negotiable metrics:

- **Income**
- **Profit**
- **Cash**

You need to know these. I'm sorry, but you just do.

There is a famous saying that incorporates all these figures:

Turnover is vanity, profit is sanity, but cash is king.

Wherever you are in your business journey, having a handle on these three figures will be an excellent place to start in your quest for financial control. Because when you start reviewing how much you are spending, and on what, you will have a much clearer idea of what is working for you, and what you should do next.

Income

What income you generate depends largely on the way that your business works, the services you offer, and what time you have available to complete the work ready to get invoiced.

Putting some thought into this at each stage of the process throughout this book will give you more raw information that you can work with, and make it easier to tweak things as you grow or change your business structure.

This includes recording the income as it comes in, having an awareness of where it comes from (particularly in terms of how it's physically received), and what your income pipeline for the future looks like.

Reviewing what your income patterns have been over the last 12 months is the place to start; how much of this is regular income? How far into the future is that income likely to continue?

If you have some projects or launches planned, what are your expectations for income from that?

Look at your business bank accounts, as well as sources such as PayPal accounts and online payment facilities. Don't forget to include these in your potential pipeline, as well as income from other sources, such as book royalties and passive income channels.

We'll look more at putting a strategy together around your income in the Solutions chapter, but for now, just an awareness of your income, and clear and full recording of it, is the main goal.

Profit

Profit is the figure that is left when you have deducted all the costs involved in running your business. The balance is real when it comes to earning the amount you want to earn to cover your costs, the tax liability and what you want to pay yourself.

Having an awareness of your costs will stem from your book-keeping records and your bank statements. There is no simpler way to do this; what are you spending money on in your business and are you getting value from each of the items you are paying for? For example:

- Subscriptions – do you actually use them? Are they needed?
- Memberships – do you utilise the support being offered, is this something that you need to continue paying?
- Advertising/marketing/networking costs – what is the return on investment that you are getting on these costs? What sort of clients do you want to work with, and does this strategy reach them? How could this be switched up to give you more of what you want?
- Any freelance consultants and support staff that you have – are you making the most of their expertise? What effort/time does it take for you to manage these relationships, or are you able to leave them to their own devices? (Sometimes looking at the monetary cost of something isn't the only consideration – be aware of the time cost to you for managing them).

Work through all your expenses, and get curious. After a deep dive like this, you may well find that it's possible to make savings on things that you don't utilise. Notice how much you are able to save, as it's very easy when you're busy to allow regular payments and subscriptions to creep up.

This is a useful exercise to do on a regular basis, for both your business and your personal finances. Do you know what you spend on a regular basis? Shining a light on where your money goes brings awareness and the opportunity to question it. Does it take you closer to your overall goal?

Cashflow

You need to be in control of your cashflow. It's as simple as that.

It's all very well and good invoicing for all the amazing work that you're doing for your clients, but another matter entirely if that cash never actually makes it into your bank account, or not in time to be able to cover the regular payments out of your business.

Cashflow management starts with knowledge and understanding.

Ideally, we need to get your income to a point where it is consistent and regularly coming in. This will help with managing your supplier payments, as well as when you can pay yourself. This will enable you to plan with certainty.

Stabilising your costs will help with being able to build up a surplus balance in the bank for when cash coming in is a little leaner. The most common thing I see is clients taking a nice bonus after a big chunk of cash comes in. This is fine, if your cashflow can take it. By looking ahead at what costs you've got coming up, and anticipated income, you will know the answer to that question. We'll cover how to use these numbers to build a cashflow forecast in the Solutions chapter.

The best foundations to help you with this is to make yourself a schedule and ensure the following gets done every month.

1. Know what work you have coming up each month, and have this noted as far ahead in advance as you can.
2. Make sure you have time scheduled to both plan and complete the work, as well as communicate with your clients so that they feel in the loop. This is Timetabling in action.
3. Based on milestones that you can agree with your clients, you'll know when you can invoice. You can automate this if you use accounting software, so make life easy for yourself. Automate the process to take your involvement (and any emotion attached to invoicing) out of the picture.
4. If you don't have milestone payments incorporated into your work plans with your clients, then consider this going forward. This can be built into the contract based on parts of the project delivered, or it can be invoiced on a monthly or bi-monthly basis if you bill based on the time you spend on a project.
5. Managing the expectations of the clients so that they know when they can expect bills and when they are expected to be paid is all part of the customer journey, so keeping them in the loop, and ensuring the lines of communication are open to highlight any problems or hiccups will reduce the chance of missed or late payments.
6. Make the credit control process as simple for yourself as you can; invoice regularly, make your payment terms clear, and have a few pre-prepared emails lined up in a sequence for when payments are late. Make them impersonal, factual, polite, but to the point. Often, people pay late because it's not at the forefront of their

mind, so a reminder is all that's needed. Assume the best, but prepare for the worst.

7. Effective credit control is a must, and accounting software can really help with this, aside from delegating the whole function! Using a package like Xero, for example, will highlight for you when an invoice is due, and when it hasn't been paid.

Being prepared for your tax bill

As the famous saying goes, there's nothing as certain as death and taxes. Having to pay tax means we're making a profit, so there is a silver lining to this cloud! By the same token, not taking the time to plan for a tax bill is foolhardy in the extreme. It's not as though HMRC are going to forget where you live!

A common scenario I hear goes something like this:

A person starts off in business on the first contract; perhaps they jumped from a corporate role, and grabbed the opportunity of a corporate contract with both hands. The money comes in and it all feels like a bit of a blur. No one pays tax in their first year, right, so that money gets swallowed up, somewhere, somehow.

A year later, approaching their first year-end, and the time has just evaporated. It's been hard work, and a holiday is definitely in order. And some nice new clothes, and that handbag too. There's a tax liability on the horizon somewhere, but not for ages yet.

Fast forward another six months and it's time to get serious about that tax bill that will need to be paid in the next 3 months or so. Accounts need to be sorted, but surely that won't take long. There haven't been many invoices, and it should be easy enough to find everything… No need to rush really. Besides, the next contract has just started.

And then the realisation starts to dawn.

The business expenses aren't much at all because it's impossible to track them down. There was definitely that workshop I paid for, but which card was used to pay for it again? Surely, they will be on email, somewhere. Pretty much all of the main expenses in the early days were just salary and dividends. Those, and getting the garden done, and converting the garage into a gym…

All the ways that you pay yourself all count as dividends if the payments haven't gone through the payroll and been taxed first. And if you can't track your expenses and the receipts, there's no evidence of the expense being tax-deductible. Suddenly, there's a £5,000 tax bill to pay. By next week. And, right now, there's £1,100 in the business account. You know there's money due in, but you don't know when those clients will pay…

And this is a whole stressful situation that could have been avoided. Does any of this sound familiar?

So, instead we make a plan where you can take the thought and emotion out of the entire process. From day one, if we can, or right now will do, if not.

As the famous Chinese proverb goes, the best time to plant a tree was 20 years ago. The second best time is now.

Depending on your level of expenses, you should be putting to one side between 10%-15% of your income to cover the corporation tax, which is currently 19%. It is regularly reviewed by HMRC, so keep an eye on what the current rate is. By ringfencing this out of the way when the money comes in, into either a separate bank account, or a bank space in one of the online banks, you will have a savings pot ready for when the bills come in.

Over time, you will be able to refine this percentage. The more data that you record in your business, the more you will know about the typical patterns in terms of income and profits, which lead directly to the tax amounts, so the better you can plan for this.

This will be a different calculation if you operate your business as a sole trader; aim at around the 10%-15% for basic rate tax payers, or 25% for higher rate tax payers (there is a cap on National insurance, which is why the percentage isn't a straight multiple of two).

Again, this should be tweaked depending on your actual business, but anything that you are putting away is going to help towards your tax bills, and is far better than nothing saved in advance at all.

Don't forget that income tax will need to be planned for on dividend payments that you take for yourself as a shareholder of your own company. (Directors manage the business and take a salary, shareholders own the business and take a share of the profits; for small companies, such as yours, you are likely to have both of these roles).

There is currently a dividend allowance available, which is tax-free, and then basic rate income tax is applied of 7.5%, and 32.5% as a higher rate tax payer, so make sure that you are ringfencing this for your tax bill. (Tax rates change year on year, so keep an eye on these, or ask for professional guidance).

If you are VAT registered, this is another thing to consider. Because whilst we may invoice the amount for our goods and services, and receive it into our bank account, the total amount received is not all ours! Where VAT is concerned, we are effectively acting as an interim tax collector, so for each invoice that we send out and get paid for, we need to be ringfencing the VAT element and keeping it to one side in a separate account too.

Tackling it this way creates a useful savings pot, as you will be able to offset your input VAT that you'll pay for some of your expenses before it's paid to HMRC. So, you will never be under-prepared for a VAT bill again! As the dates for this will be timetabled in, following on from the Timetabling chapter, you will be well ahead of the curve, and not need to worry about this from a cashflow point of view either.

By taking control and planning the time in, we will be empowered to make decisions with the cash that is left.

Speaking of VAT...

All VAT returns now fall under the Making Tax Digital remit, which means that you have to have digital accounting software to be able to file the returns, or as a minimum, bridging software to connect your spreadsheets to HMRC's filing system.

I recommend accounting software for various reasons; it connects directly to your bank feed. It minimises errors by downloading transactions for you automatically. They can be used for budgeting and forecasting, as well as bookkeeping, so there are many more user-friendly features that you can take advantage of.

Once you have this set up, this will actually save you more time and give you more visibility of what's going on in your business, rather than a trusty spreadsheet, which needs to be manually updated. Whilst I love these, I can't tell you the number of documents I've received from clients where a formula is wrong, where several rows have been missed off on a total, or the wrong percentage has been applied. Accounting software removes that uncertainty.

If you aren't VAT registered, there's no reason you can't take on board some of these comments about bookkeeping systems. You don't have to be VAT registered to take advantage of bookkeeping software. What's more, Making Tax Digital for income tax will come into effect from April 2024, so now is a good time to get used to a new software before it becomes more of a necessity.

Other helpful tips:

Use one bank account and credit card for business purposes

Whilst you will inevitably have the odd expense for your business that you will need to reimburse yourself for, by far the easiest way of keeping track of your business costs is to run everything through one business bank account, as well as using one credit card only for business purposes.

Running your business as a limited company, as most of you will be, you'll legally need to have a separate company bank account.

But regularly paying for items out of other personal bank accounts and credit cards, without a robust expenses system in place, is a recipe for disaster:

- You'll never have a handle on what your actual business costs are
- You miss out on taking advantage of all the tax relief available to you
- You won't be able to accurately forecast the true costs and profit from running your business

It's perfectly fine to have more than one account in the company name, and indeed you should, to ringfence your tax and VAT savings like we've talked about, but make sure that you're keeping track of all your costs and expenses too.

I highly recommend making use of tools such as Hubdoc, or Dext, or other similar apps, where you can store digital copies of invoices and receipts that then integrate with your digital accounting software to save time.

Finally, I highly recommend that you don't use your business accounts as your own personal piggy bank. Your remuneration plan should cover all of this, so take some time to understand how much your business needs to pay you to cover all of your personal financial needs.

Factoring in your personal finances

Do you have a handle on how much you need to take from your business each month to cover all your own costs? Do you pay yourself the same amount each month, with regularity, that then covers all your personal financial needs?

Taking some time to get to grips with this, if you don't already, is a really useful exercise. This will help to highlight how much you need to be paying yourself on a basis regular, without the need to be dipping into the business account as you go along.

I find a good way to do this firstly is to go through your personal bank statements (Come on, you knew this was coming).

Divide all your spending up into three categories:

Need to have ¦ Nice to have ¦ Want to have

Now these will be subjective, to some extent, so allocate the costs to best suit you.

Your 'need to haves' are utilities, food and transport costs. Things you can't live without or get away with not paying.

Your 'nice to haves' might include social costs, entertaining costs, gym memberships, and the things you'd prefer not to have to manage without.

Your 'want to haves' are the treats, the luxuries, the holidays, and the extravagances.

Your income needs to cover these in the priority order for you. Knowing what these are will help you prioritise, as well as highlighting what the regular dividend payments you're aiming for might help to pay for.

Well done for getting through this chapter! If you don't deal with finances on a regular basis, this sort of stuff can make your head hurt, so be proud of yourself! If you are the sort of person that likes to have an awareness, this is perfect for you. If you delegate this side of things, keeping an eye on the key metrics for you will give you the action plan you need for improving your important metrics.

If I were to give you one piece of advice, it would be to focus on your cashflow forecasting. By having a strategy and a plan for what income you want to come in, and when, you can manage the following from this one task:

- Budgeting your spending.
- Planning your salary/dividends.
- Setting aside enough for your tax liability.
- Knowing when you have potential income gaps ahead of time, so you can do something about them.
- Planning marketing and social media strategies to highlight your upcoming business offerings and launches.

I'll cover how to pull together a forecast in the next chapter, Solutions.

Most importantly, it allows you to be PROACTIVE in your business, instead of reactive. This should be the sole motivation for anyone to want to have a handle on their finances for running their business, and by extension, helping them to live the life they want in the shortest time possible.

8

SOLUTIONS

So far in our journey, we've covered off the foundations. I've talked about the steps I took to get myself to a place of feeling in control financially, as well as sharing more detail and resources about how you can do it too.

Please don't underestimate this work. I found these tricky to do, and they took years to get right for me, let alone feel confident enough to think that I could share these with you. If they helped me as much as they did, there must be others out there who could benefit too, right?

This section of the book is more about decision making, and this is different for everyone. It will depend on where you are up to in your business and life journey, how you run your business and what you want to achieve.

Essentially, the plan is to establish what your North Star is before we can then come up with a flight plan to get you there in the shortest time possible. And that's exactly what you're capable of doing now. You have all of the pieces; you've looked at the numbers, you've looked at your time, you've considered all of your resources and you're working on your mindset (trust me, this will be a lifelong process!). Now what?

If you've reached this point in the book and you don't have an idea of what your North Star is, now is the time to start dreaming.

North Star Exercise

OK, so what is it all about for you? We don't go into business on our own for the good of our health, there is always something that triggers it. A fleeting dream, an aspiration, a goal, a glass ceiling you saw someone smash. Why not you?

What inspired you to go all out and work for yourself? It isn't easy on this journey; being taken seriously when you 'work from home.' Dealing with the 'it's OK for you, you work from home so you can take time off whenever you want' comments from well-meaning but stressed-out friends.

Dealing with all the areas we've talked about in this book is a lot of pressure, as well as managing your pipeline, strategy and finding time for yourself in there somewhere too.

I'm not talking about how much you want to earn this year, or how many hours you want to work. These are the building blocks that we can use to help pave the way to your North Star. But to start laying the bricks for that path, we need to know what direction we're travelling in.

So, what is it?

Try sitting quietly for a short while, take some time out, maybe first thing in the morning when you can find some peace just for you. Picture yourself twenty years from now (or at a time in the future when you think you'll know you've made it – again, this is different for everyone).

Feel into who you are at that point in time. Where do you live? What are you wearing? Who is with you? What is your family structure now? Do you have children? More children? Grandchildren? What does your work life look like? Have you retired by now? What does your other half do? What kind of lifestyle do you live? How does it feel to have 'made it'?

What does that look like for you?

Have you sold your successful business and are you now living a comfortable life off the proceeds?

Have you brought your children into the business, which you've kept a controlling share in, and are now living off regular dividend income and keeping involved in a non-executive capacity?

Have you sold up the family home and moved to a property by the sea, or moved abroad? Where are you living?

Have you retired your other half and given them the freedom to work on what they love, while you continue to consult in your business, having brought in a team of skilled upstarts who are running the business for you?

How will you know when you've made it, and what does that look like?

Once you've got the image in your head, you have the North Star that we're aiming for. What that looks like financially, and how long it's going to take to get there, is the next step.

What's your number?

Now we have a destination, we have the bones of a plan. So now we can get practical about what we need to have in place. To live that life, how much would that take?

At this stage, you don't need exact figures, but you can make an estimated guess on the cost of your dream lifestyle annually. What are your regular bills likely to be? How much will your car take to run? How much support do you want to continue to give your children, and your grandchildren? How much do you want to have stashed away? Let's start putting the meat on the bones of this idea.

Having this plan in place now, and using your business as a vehicle to get you closer to where you want to be, will give you a direction right now. How much cash do you have available to be investing in savings, investments, and pensions?

How much is your home worth, and could this be leveraged to get you closer to where you want to be somewhere down the line? Does your business support your current lifestyle, as well as the plans you want to make for your future self? What changes would you need to make in order for that to be possible?

Here we get realistic about what we want now and what we want most. Somewhere, we need to join the dots between how things are at the moment, and how we plot our flight plan to get where we want to be.

What other sources of income do you have, and are you making the most of each of these? Are you taking full advantage of tax efficiencies and not overpaying income tax for the profits that you're extracting from your business? Are you operating your business through the most tax efficient vehicle, and when do you know it's the right time to change?

It is likely that this flight plan will involve a number of different strategies. I like to picture this as all being building blocks that individually stand alone as an action plan, but when combined make up the bigger picture.

This might include owning investment property, building up your own business and exploring ways of working smarter instead of harder, building different streams of income, including passive income, as well as investing in different savings and investment strategies.

Do any of these sound like a bit of something you might quite like?

Which do you think you can start to put into action now?

What might stop you from achieving them, or potentially even getting started? Are they real blocks, or are they perceived blocks? (Remember the Mindset chapter).

At some point soon, it would be sensible to meet an independent financial adviser. Someone who can hear your dreams and know which products will get you where you want to be even sooner. Someone who can secure the mortgage for your dream house when a high-street bank won't touch you because you're self-employed. I'm not that person, as I can't advise on products, but I can point you in the right direction, so get in touch with me if you'd like to learn more about this and you don't have a trusted adviser of your own – tanya@financialwingwoman.com. Not only can they help with the finer details of the plan, you can also explore products with them that will get you where you want to be in the best possible way for you and your attitude to risk.

Practical solutions – the next steps

We all need tools; we all need guidance. But, as I've said a few times now at different points in this book, we don't know what we don't know.

In this section, I'm going to give you the seven key action steps I took, and the same action that I guide my clients with to this day, to get quantifiable results. This draws on everything we've covered so far, so hang on to your hats!

1) Building your business into a slick machine

In the Accountability chapter, I talked about what actually needs to be done in your business. I recommended that the best way to figure this out is to map out your customer journey.

If you haven't done this yet, or need to find the time to give this exercise the space it deserves, this is your permission to take action. Block out an afternoon, half a day, some time at the weekend, whenever you know you can dedicate some uninterrupted time for this, and roll up your sleeves with some big sheets of paper and coloured pens. If ever there was an excuse to let your creative inner version of you loose, this is it. Go on, I dare you!

You need to write as much detail as you can for each touch point with your client and each time when action is needed by you. When you've finished, at a later point in time, you can highlight the parts you love to do, the parts you can't be excused from, and the parts that you could easily delegate as you go, but this isn't the primary purpose of this exercise.

This part is about spending some time understanding what needs to be done at each stage. In as much detail as possible.

How does a client reach out to you? What platforms do they use? What places can they find you? Is it your website or your social media profiles? Get specific.

What happens next? How do you respond? What action options do you give them? Write out pro-forma responses, whether for an email or on a messaging application, such as Facebook Messenger or WhatsApp. Writing out a response, and saving this as a keyboard shortcut on your phone, or as a standard email, will take any thought required out of that action step. Automate this, and you don't need to get involved.

If the next step is to book in for a call, automate the link for your digital calendar so they can choose a slot that works for both you and them, at a time when you're available. No input from you will be required, and at any point in the future, should you choose to delegate any of the administration, someone else can oversee this for you.

The point is that you have written out what happens, at what stage in the process, and exactly how you want it to look. This can be tweaked and improved at a later date, but for now, you are documenting everything that is in your head and freeing up the space. You have a blueprint.

- Write your standard emails, and leave space for personalisation, if that's called for.
- Have terms of business and contracts already drafted up as template, which simply then need to be tailored and sent out.
- Write checklists to make sure all parts of the process are covered off, in the right order.

Whilst this will be time consuming to start with, it is an exercise that will give you the foundations of how your business is run. At a point in the future, when you choose to delegate parts of this process (because, let's face it, you know this is where we're headed, right?!) to be managed by someone else, it will be as simple as sharing the relevant documents and they will have a full standard operating procedure document to follow. It won't be in your head any more, it can be compartmentalised and outsourced.

Not only will this give you the foundations you need to effectively run your business, you'll also be able to identify where bottlenecks are present and where efficiency can be improved. The visual nature of creating the customer journey path will make this easier to see.

2) Using automation and outsourcing to your advantage

If automation and delegation isn't something you've done before, I completely understand the hesitation and reluctance to try something new. Especially if you're already busy and juggling all the things.

Checking that a new system is working, testing it, or checking up on someone else, even just to start with, can feel as though you're just making that to-do list even longer. Have faith though, this really is where the magic happens, if scaling your business and giving yourself more time back is something you genuinely want to explore.

I struggled for the longest time because of the control aspect. I'd spent time (read: hours and hours, and painstaking hours) growing my business and nurturing my clients; the last thing I wanted was to bring someone else into my business for them to wreck all my effort so far. Or for me to set up automation emails that bombarded and upset a client, or make a mistake with something.

But that's all part of the due diligence process of automation and outsourcing. This isn't something that you'll jump into with both feet, you'll explore the options first. We all know you're smart, and you'll also likely know by now what your work capacity looks like, but to expand your offering and scale your business, things need to change.

As part of working through the customer journey, you will clearly have identified the different touch points with your clients on the whole journey of working with you.

Project management tools, such as Asana, and customer relationship management software, such as Dubsado, can automate this process for you, and integrate with functions such as scheduling calls, setting up video call links and even invoicing within your bookkeeping system.

Using technology such as Otter to record client meetings means that you can email a transcription and/or voice recording of the call to all parties and share the action points that you've agreed on without having to remember yourself.

Tools such as Trello and Motion help to prioritise your own time and to do list and help you to maximise what needs to get done in a day.

Getting the processes out of your head is the first step towards freeing up your capacity for working on the parts of your business that light you up, and that are in your zone of genius, as explained by Gay Hendricks in his book, The Big Leap. Spending your time on comfortable admin won't help you, but automation will and personally, I found it incredibly useful while I was still nervous about outsourcing and letting other people near my clients.

Ask trusted contacts what software and apps they use, and also ask for recommendations of who is in the know for help with systems to keep everything aligned and avoid duplicating your efforts, or causing unnecessary hassle.

Outsourcing is a different ball game altogether, but again is something that needs to happen if growing and scaling your business is all part of the bigger picture of achieving your North Star.

As you already have your customer journey mapped out now, you can identify the parts of the process that you might like to outsource. The admin parts, the technical parts, the time-consuming parts; get creative, put your CEO hat on and consider whether you should be the person to be doing all these aspects of your business.

Ask around again for recommendations; who are your trusted contacts and peers using? What do they get help with, and how has it changed and improved their business?

Start small with tasks that are easily managed. Perhaps accountancy and bookkeeping are something you could outsource. Marketing and social media management could be something else. Administration and time management could be high on your list; ask yourself which are the parts of your business that you would happily never do again if you could get away with it. That's where you start!

Building up the trust to bring someone into your inner circle will help you elevate your game massively. Allowing that someone to take all the things that are spinning around in your head and free up that capacity and energy will totally change your business. Baby steps are fine, but keep remembering your position as the CEO. Picture her in your mind, and think about the action you need to take to get there.

You can start small when it comes to doing this. You don't want this to be a source of overwhelm, as it's intended to help you.

Perhaps start with hiring a virtual assistance to do 10 hours a month for you and assign to them the tasks that you absolutely hate with a passion, which could free up 2-3 hours a week for you, and see how it goes.

How much time have you wasted trying to format a word document so that your logo sits right at the top of the page?

How much time have you faffed trying to put a 'simple' design together in Canva because it's supposedly really 'straightforward to use,' but then lost count of how many times the different boxes keep moving to the front and covering up what you're trying to achieve? (Can you tell I'm talking from experience here?)

Were they all necessary tasks for your business, and are you the best person for the job?

As with all things that need nurturing and feeding and growing, it takes a village, and running your business is no different, no matter how protective you feel about it being all yours.

Sometimes we can get so lost in where we are and what habits and patterns we've created that we don't notice we aren't working as efficiently as we could be. Our time isn't being utilised to maximum capacity, a bit like our money too sometimes!

3) Using your current financials to build realistic forecasts and strategies

You know what's coming here, don't you? We talked about this in the Housekeeping chapter under both the Profit and Cashflow sections. This is where you are going to need to get intimate with your bank statements and your bookkeeping system. You knew it was coming, don't groan at me! In order to be able to forecast with confidence, and build an ongoing business development strategy from these numbers, you're going to have to make sure they're both up to date and accurate.

If you have an accountant that does this for you, then great. Get them on board by explaining your goal and ask how they can support you with this. They could take the whole task off your plate, or else they could give you more guidance on how you go about doing this for yourself.

I like to prepare forecasts in the reverse order; I start with costs instead of income. The choice is up to you, but I like to be able to clearly see what the outgoings are for a business, build up a full picture, and then map out the income that will cover (to 'break even') and exceed the spends.

Set aside the time for this exercise, and be brutally honest with what it costs to run your business. Check your recent bank statements, perhaps going back three months if a larger period feels too much, and plot your monthly costs. You are going to need a wider view at some point, because you're likely to have some costs that are paid annually. This is where your bookkeeping system will help you – review your suppliers to jog your memory of that Zoom subscription or your business insurance renewal that is only paid once a year.

Two key elements that you need to also include in here are your costs, as in the amount that you pay yourself (salary and dividends, along with any pension payments and benefits in kind), as well as the tax you'll need to pay on your profits. We'll cover what you pay yourself and how best to tax efficiently do this later in this chapter, but ringfencing your tax liability as you go along is also something we've mentioned before. This is a cost of doing business and it should be budgeted for as such.

Prepare your forecast for the year ahead, with costs down the side and months across the top, and drop the relevant numbers into your spreadsheet. For a template, check out the book resource section of my website (link in the last chapter).

You now have a clear picture of the breakeven point of your business; exactly what you need to make each month to cover your outgoings.

Next, you can add your income to the equation. List each of your different services, offerings, and intended launches down the side. Drop in the income figures that you know, making sure you take care to include the income based on when you are relatively certain of when the cash will be received.

If you're using the template I've provided, the cash summary at the top of the spreadsheet will make clear where you have any cashflow gaps that need your attention. If you're not, this simply summarises the cash position at the beginning and end of each month, taking into account what you are expecting to come in and out of your bank account. You only need to input your starting cash position at the start of the period you're covering to make this work.

From this place in your workings, you can create more concrete plans for when you plan to launch your offerings and services, how you plan to structure your marketing and social media content plan and other aspects of your business strategy. This might include staff planning and resource allocation, and booking other experts or support staff.

This is also a perfect way to simulate the future earnings and what you want to be able to draw from the company to pay yourself as well as to cover savings plans, pension contributions and the like. With an aspirational new salary and maximum pension contributions coming out of the business, how much would you need to earn to cover it? This model would tell you exactly that.

This model would also tell you what the realistic tax liabilities would be on a monthly basis, which you can use to ringfence the cash to one side to prepare for your tax bill as you go along. By saving the VAT as the money comes in too, you will never be surprised by a tax bill again. Welcome to financial control!

4) Windows of Opportunity - WOO

In this day and age of chasing the next new sparkly thing, or being guided by a mentor/coach to steer your business in a certain direction, it is easy to lose sight of what's right in front of you. Back in the days when things felt tight for me, I found that the most successful quick cashflow injections I could arrange came from clients I already worked with who perhaps didn't know (because I hadn't told them) all of the services that I offered.

With a detailed understanding of your cashflow and where your income comes from, you too can create a plan from your windows of opportunity before thinking about expanding and connecting with new clients. I'm not saying don't do that; you absolutely should. But make things easy for yourself; we're working smarter, not harder, right?

This exercise doesn't need to be done from a place of scarcity, like it once was for me. This is about adopting a CEO approach to running your business. What do you already have in place in your business, what resources do you have at your disposal, and how could you further help the clients you already work with?

Creating and building relationships with new clients is expensive and labour intensive. When I was spending hours networking in person back in 2010, it was estimated that you needed to have around seven touch points with potential clients and contacts before they started to warm to you and would be more likely to take an interest in your communications. These days, with the development of social media and far more choices available to us, it's realistically more like twenty-seven touch points before you readily recognise someone in the field of work that you're interested in accessing. So, you need to get busy to expand your visibility network!

Or do you? By identifying your WOO, you can look a lot closer to home. This exercise involves mapping out all your services, and identifying which clients, current and former, have made use of which over the years. Assuming there is a genuine need for what you have to offer – remember, selling isn't sleazy if you approach clients and potential clients from a place of offering help for a problem they need solving – then this can form part of your **communication strategy;** to touch base with your existing and potential clients and make them aware of the services you have to offer.

Looking at this from a different perspective, with each of your services mapped out, you can see how many clients have taken advantage of each over time. If you have a large portion of clients not aware of certain services that you offer it could be that they simply aren't aware of everything you offer. This could indicate a gap in your **marketing strategy,** which should become some-thing you could focus on, again, as a form of low hanging fruit. Check your website and touch points to update this information, and make use of social media to create awareness around it.

There is a simple matrix template in the book resources section of my website (link in the final chapter) that you are free to download to help you with this. Go and get stuck in and let me know how you get on!

5) Paying yourself tax efficiently

If you operate as a sole trader this section won't apply to you, but is something you should definitely consider incorporating your business for, even if this is the sole reason for it. Operating through a limited company, assuming that your profits are at a sufficient level of around £50,000 per year, gives you the flexi-bility to choose the level of salary that you can draw from your own company, and the level of dividends that you take as well, provided the profits are there to support it.

Dividends as a remuneration strategy are advantageous as they are taxed at a lower rate than salary payments, and also aren't liable to National Insurance either. The distinction is a subtle one, and one that needs due caution when it comes to dealing with HMRC.

Salary is a reward for employment and services performed under those duties, and is also subject to employment law. Dividends, on the other hand, are a return on an investment, by way of share ownership, and are dependent upon sufficient profits being available for paying out.

The difference between the two can have a big impact, but because the dividends aren't allowable as a tax-deductible expense, the payment of corporation tax will be higher instead. Payments of dividends need to be managed carefully as if they are seen to be remuneration amounts (for example, by being paid monthly, or several times a month, in much the same way a salary would be paid), HMRC could view these payments as salary payments and decide to tax them as such.

Comparing different salary levels and dividend amounts, and working out the tax for each scenario, is the only way to know what the overall impact would be. A higher dividend amount would increase the corporation tax due, so your strategy needs to be balanced across all the taxes that you're exposed to.

Looking at a simple view of this, with a turnover/income of £100,000, and costs of £18,000, taking a director salary of £12,570 out of the company, which is the current income tax personal allowance, and the rest of your personal income as dividends, you would be around £2,000 better off at the end of the year by running this business through a limited company.

It's important to highlight that this isn't the same outcome for all scenarios, so I would definitely recommend running your own numbers for this with your own figures, or taking individual professional advice for your own circumstances before making a decision on this.

Other remuneration options to consider would be benefits in kind through your company, and the tax relief available by making pension contributions into a company pension scheme.

Whilst benefits in kind might not be viewed as a salary substitute by you, they are by HMRC, so this is the simplest way to picture the tax implications. You can use the company funds to pay for any private expenses, provided that the tax is accounted for correctly. For example, you could pay for private school fees through the company, or nursery fees, or private medical insurance, or all three! (cashflow permitting). As the individual benefitting from this payment, you would be taxed as though you had taken that payment as additional salary, which is essentially what a benefit in kind is.

Your tax liability would be higher, but you would save by not physically needing to pay for the school fees out of your own pocket from your 'net' salary.

Pension contributions are a very tax efficient way of providing for your future self, which is a necessary consideration when it comes to putting together your flight plan, but this wouldn't be cash you could access easily before reaching 55, as the current guidance allows. Only invest substantial cash in a pension if you are certain that the cash won't be required in the near future.

As with all advice, it's vital that you consider all options, so professional advice would be recommended in order to ensure you're considering all points that might impact you. Making a plan for your earning potential, and determining that your salary might be lower to avoid paying tax won't be helpful, for example, if you're planning to obtain new mortgage financing in the next few years, as proof of your earnings over perhaps three business periods will be required, along with affordability calculations. This is a prime example of knowing and considering all your needs before taking action.

6) Building up reserves for a rainy day

If you don't have an emergency fund, then now is the perfect time to start working towards building one. As you'll have so much of your finances and the inner workings of your business now more streamlined, this could be something that you can quickly and easily get set up and forget about.

When I was struggling with the mountain of debt I needed to pay back, I made the mistake initially of paying every spare penny I had off the balance of a credit card, as my goal was to eliminate this as quickly as I could. But all that meant was that when an inevitable unexpected bill came in, or the car service was more than I was expecting, I had to use a credit card to cover it as I had no cash reserves. This led to feeling as though I was always being knocked back in my progress against my debt.

Once I realised I needed to have an emergency fund, I turned my attention to building up a cash reserve as a starting point, as well as paying down my debt, albeit a bit slower to start with. For me, this was when a switch flicked in my mind.

I started to find ways in managing my cash flow to both save a small amount, as well as pay down my debt. Instead of wanting to reward myself for a hard week with a bottle of wine, the motivator became saving and watching that pot grow. Whilst I only saved a small amount – 1% of my income to start with – this was enough to plant a seed of hope for me, that I could watch grow over time.

I initially focused on paying my minimum payments on my credit cards, and reaching £1,000 in savings as an emergency. Once I had that pot, I returned my focus back to the debt repayments.

I chose to focus on paying as much as I could against the debt that cost me the most, in terms of interest being charged. Once I'd paid that off, I used the payments I had been paying against that card and added that to the minimum payments I was making against the next most expensive card. Do you follow? A snowball effect happened; the more I paid off, the more I had to be able to pay off.

Whilst juggling debt with the need to save may not be an issue that you struggle with, the principles of starting small with saving to give yourself some liquid security is something we can all learn from.

To save £1,000, you need to first reach £100. To save £100 you need to first reach £10. Every big dream starts small, and it's no different with savings. And whilst your income may regularly come in, the path to financial independence starts with providing for that version of your future self that you're aiming for.

Now, when I talk to my clients about savings, we talk about three forms of saving; these include funds that are readily accessible in (likely) low interest bank accounts. I recommend having around three to six months' worth of costs saved in an easily accessible bank, should an emergency arise.

I would also recommend a pension pot. Depending upon earnings, you can save up to £40,000 a year (under current guidelines) into your personal pension, which all contributes to the funds available to you in retirement. Whilst these funds aren't accessible until you reach a certain age, they form part of a balanced overall financial plan for your future independence.

In between these two, I would recommend an investing pot. By balancing an accessible cash fund (that will unlikely be making much of any interest) with a plan for a retirement fund baking nicely, you have a space in the middle that you can get creative with. Including this alongside a savings and pension pot, depending on your personal cash position, offers one key benefit; compound interest. Even with a small starting pot, over time, compound interest will mean that the amount invested will steadily increase, so the earlier this starts, the better. Once you have your six-month buffer saved, you could focus on increasing the amount you add into your investing pot.

This could then be used to invest directly with companies of interest if you have enough confidence for this. Alternatively, you could invest in a stocks and shares ISA, as an example, to be able to access an investing fund yourself. Ideally, you would need to speak to a trusted financial adviser to help you put this plan together for you for your overall financial needs, and I certainly can't advise what products you should invest in, but the three pots principal is a sure-fire way to build up reserves that you can rely on and give you financial control.

As I've mentioned a couple of times, when it comes to making a choice of which products are best for you, seek the advice of an independent financial adviser to make the best selection for you and your circumstances. Ultimately, the goal is to get your money working as efficiently for you as possible, so this is a worthwhile exercise! Investing is a form of passive income, if done right. That growth, over time, will form part of your overall plan for your North Star.

Watching your savings and investing funds grow over time becomes addictive; it beats adding up credit card statements any day! Every now and then, check in on what these are worth, cumulatively. What is your 'net worth'? To get this technically right, you'd also need to knock off your debt total, but watching this figure grow over time was what helped me to remember that any sacrifice I made was totally worth it for my future self.

7) Working on building additional income streams

Streamlining and building efficiencies in your business together are the key elements of building stable foundations. They will give you the confidence you need for making decisions and will save you bags of time, I promise, once the work is done (it might not feel like it in the moment, but it is worth it!). You will become more agile, and be able to make quicker decisions. Imagine your dream client approaches you; can you handle it? Do you have the capacity to take on the work? Do you know? Or do you have to go away and think about things? This process will show you that you can; not only that, but you'll know exactly the changes you can implement to make it happen. From here on in, you can keep the wheels turning and focus on scaling your business and growth.

Adding more services, increasing capacity, and bringing on board staff and associates will help you get there, but what if there was a simpler way to start with?

Generating additional income streams with what you already know was a revelation to me. Back when I first started, testing the waters and building this system, meant I had to take on more work. As I'd just started on my own, with my own practice, that was fine because I'd resigned from my corporate role, so I had time. I added back in some financial training commitments for a number of days a year to make the income up, as well as expanding my network again.

I had other contacts in the accountancy world, so I reached out to representatives of a few of the accountancy institutes and was able to utilise my financial training knowledge by working on the academic side of accounting, which I still do to this day.

More recently, I've branched out to use social media to raise awareness of the work I do. This is predominantly to educate and share my financial coaching knowledge, but it has led to more opportunities for me. This book, for example, is evidence of that. You're reading it, which is great, how did you hear about it?

Additional sources of income create financial security. If you are unable to work, for any reason, or one area of your business is affected by something unexpected, like a pandemic, you will always have something else to fall back on. How would it feel to pandemic-proof your business?

If you want to be even smarter, you can find a way to do this in a passive or semi-passive way. A way that doesn't eat up more of your time. We don't want to be trading more of that, the whole point of this book was to help you streamline what you're doing, but what if you could find a way to share your genius with others on a bigger scale? By operating through a one-to-few or one-to-many business model instead of a one-to-one model.

If you have specialised knowledge in an area that few know about, you could create an online course or workshop to share your mad skills. Speaking to 20 people, or 50 people (come on, with technology, the sky's the limit here) who each pay you individually for you to deliver something once, imagine the possibilities. Not only can you earn a stack more for less of your time, think about all the people you could help and impact too. And in a much faster timeframe than if you line them all up to help them individually.

Fancy ramping that up a notch? Run another workshop, or course. Sell it again. Record it. You know how automation works now, automate the selling part of this. Create a link on your website and offer this for sale. And now you have a source of passive income.

Write about what you do and monetise it. Where do you think I got the idea for this book? Once written, it's done. And it can sell again and again. You can do that. Remember that North Star? These suggestions can all form part of the flight plan to get you there.

I could have written continuously here; shared with you the mistakes I made (there were many!) and how my path might not be the right path for you. But my goal is to inspire and show you the possibilities if you just give yourself permission to dream. Know that you can do anything you set your mind to when you put your CEO hat on and adopt a Solutions approach to finding your own path. I don't have any regrets; I'm grateful that the path I chose ultimately led me to here, and that's what I wish for you, dear reader.

This is the end of the MATHS® system, but not quite the end of this book. I would love to hear from you when you have implemented any of the steps in this chapter. Tag me in your social media posts, email me directly on tanya@ financialwingwoman.com. I would love to feature your success stories in the updated version of this book at some point, so come and say hello!

9

THE NEXT STEPS IN YOUR JOURNEY

Well, you did it! I can't tell you how unbelievably happy it makes me that you've made it this far and you're reading this last chapter.

It's taken me several months to get to grips with writing this book, whilst battling my own inner imposter, not to mention overthinking about sharing my personal story with you. But ultimately, I wanted to show you that no-one is perfect. No-one has it all together, all of the time. And I think more of us need to be honest about this. Because as we grow, we'll always face new things. So, will we ever be 100% certain that we're always doing the right thing? Probably not.

For me, it had to boil down to what is really important to me and then I knew I had to focus on that. I want to make sure there is someone shouting about financial independence for all. When I picture you, I picture a woman, not too dissimilar to me. You just don't have the financial background I do. And that didn't always do me a fat lot of good, as you now know! I want to speak to women just like you, mostly because I relate to the struggle, the uncertainty and those questions in your head going round and round. But I also know it doesn't have to be that way.

We are often disadvantaged when it comes to expectations of what we are capable of. It's that whole mindset piece that's so important; we watch our role models from when we're small. We go to school and pick up more examples of how things 'should be done'. I know this isn't always the case now, but in my primary school days, the girls did needlework and copied out the lyrics from Smash Hits magazine, while the boys did woodwork and simulated killing each other in epic battle scenes on the school field. It was stereotyped. And some of that will always stay with us.

Financial education and awareness needs to change, and the taboo of talking about money is also something that has no place in today's society. The landscape is shifting, but it's not enough. We need to do more. True financial independence comes from the inherent belief that you always have a choice. It's about never having to stay in a relationship or a job simply because you can't afford to leave. It's about knowing you have the power to live this life on your own terms. And run your business the way you want to.

Because this is about so much more than money. Because it's only money, at the end of the day. We've learned in this book that there are other, more valuable, and non-renewable resources that we can't always control, but we can influence. So, we need to remember that we have the power we need all along.

Our time.

Our mindset.

Financial independence comes with knowledge. It comes with taking the blinkers off and releasing all limiting beliefs that have kept you 'safe' so far. You are your security blanket now, so you don't need those any more.

So, the purpose of this book now is to empower you to pull all of that knowledge together, combine it with your own drive, genius and ambition, and set a course for your own flight plan and really soar.

And like that favourite pair of jeans, the more you work on it and refer back to your plan, checking in on your progress from time to time, the more comfortable it will feel.

Shining a light on your North Star

Listen, don't worry if setting your intentions for a distant spot on the horizon feels too far away. It doesn't have to be set in stone; you can set an interim destination. Like that holiday you're looking forward to on the beach, or sightseeing, or whatever it is you desire, whether it's big or small or at some point in the future. Because part of your plans need to include recharging those batteries too. So you can expand your horizons to explore the possibilities of what life could be like, but then you go back home and get back to 'normal'. Aim for that holiday as a small step. Where will you go?

As you flex your muscles and work through the exercises in this book, your confidence will grow. Why can't you plan to be scaling back the hours you work in the next ten years? Or even five years?

Hit one goal, then aim for the next. A journey around the world with a fixed destination isn't a perfect linear path, like the equator. You take detours, rest stops, and refuel the plane. The path to your North Star is like life; it will move with you. And the best journeys are the ones with the unexpected pit stops along the way, so you need to get ready to enjoy the ride!

So set your eyes on something. Put it on your vision board where you can see it. It doesn't matter if it changes later. You can't possibly predict all of the opportunities that might cross your path as you explore the possibilities that will come next, so be flexible. Acknowledge that the path might change, and be cool with it.

Your North Star is the ultimate destination, but you are working on the foundations of that path now; your flight plan. Getting those foundations in place creates a springboard for what comes next. Knowing you are on the path you want to be on for you, and that you have a helicopter view of what's going on.

And how will it feel to get there under your own steam? By not relying on one income source, or on someone else to give you that security. Empowering, that's how it will feel. You're backing you, and now all other bets are off. You are in control.

You have the MATHS® toolkit now, you have everything you need to be on your way.

Let's recap.

Mindset

You can understand what's going on in the unconscious parts of your brain now. The choices you make in the moment aren't always measured or considered so use this chapter to your advantage. Take the emotion out of your decision making by acknowledging what you need and give yourself permission to do whatever gives you control back.

Accountability

You don't need to fake it until you make it anymore. That CEO mindset was always within you, you just didn't know how to access it. Being honest about what you are best at in your business, and what you can achieve in the time you want to work, will be the next step in building your own self-respect. Boundaries galore now as you understand what you can achieve, when it can be done, and maybe, just maybe, you can accept that getting help to achieve all of these goals, isn't such a bad thing after all!

Timetabling

If this chapter hasn't removed half of what rattles around in your head, then you need to go and read it again! Making all the important dates and deadlines visible removes the power they have over you. Gone are the times when you used to wake up in the middle of the night wondering if you'd filed something on time, because it's already written down. It doesn't need to disturb you, it's in hand.

Housekeeping

Keeping your eyes on the numbers might not be something you've always done, but we've talked about how when we journey to new places, we need to take new routes. Getting comfortable with your finances will get you exactly where you want to be, so now you don't have to delegate or defer that helicopter view anymore because that's all yours to enjoy. With visibility comes the power to make strategic decisions, and that's what the CEO mindset is all about.

Solutions

How will you get there? This is how you'll get there! You have your own flight plans to implement, one step at a time. You can put them into place, check over, tweak, and improve as you go along. If something's not working as you want, then you can change it. Need more money to ramp up your plans faster? This is the chapter you'll go to to decide which button to press next. It's all here, you just have to choose which you'll go with.

Do it with me, I've got you

It's my hope that you are feeling super strong, prepared, and ready to take control of your financial destination and guess what...? The journey doesn't stop here.

Sometimes it can feel uncomfortable making big changes and implementing new things like this, especially if it's not something you've done before. I've talked about connection and keeping yourself accountable, but you don't have to do it by yourself. You can do it with me. I'll be launching MATHS® as a course later this year, so you'll be able to work through this along with me.

There are loads of other ways that you can work with me and make sure that your flight plan is guaranteed to take off. You can find all the details on my website –

www.financialwingwoman.com/work-with-me/

You can also find the resources that I refer to throughout this book on my website –

www.financialwingwoman.com/bookresources

Why me? As your Financial Wingwoman, I'm here to help you look at your finances and how you run your business in a positive way. It doesn't have to be scary, and it needs to be at the top of your to-do list if you want to build a business that works for you.

Thank you so, so much for sticking with the process. Well done you! Don't forget to stay in touch.

Lots of love

Tanya x

The Financial Wingwoman